AUTOMOTIVE DETAILI

A COMPLETE CAR CARE GUIDE FOR AUTO ENTHUSIASTS AND DETAILING PROFESSIONALS

DON TAYLOR

HPBooks

HPBooks
are published by
The Berkley Publishing Group
A member of Penguin Putnam Inc.
375 Hudson Street
New York, New York 10014

First Edition: June 1998

© 1998 Don Taylor
10 9 8 7 6 5 4 3

Library of Congress Cataloging-in-Publication Data

Taylor, Don (Donald D.)
    Automotive detailing : a complete car care guide for auto
enthusiasts and detailing professionals / Don Taylor. — 1st ed.
        p.   cm.
    ISBN 1-55788-288-6
    1. Automobile detailing.   2. Automobiles—Conservation and
restoration.   I. Title
TL 153.T315   1998
629.28'72—dc21

97-45786
CIP

Book Design & Production by Bird Studios
Interior photos by the author unless otherwise noted
Cover photos by Michael Lutfy

NOTICE: The information in this book is true and complete to the best of our knowledge. All recommendations on parts and procedures are made without any guarantees on the part of the author or the publisher. Tampering with, altering, modifying or removing any emissions-control device is a violation of federal law. Author and publisher disclaim all liability incurred in connection with the use of this information.

would like to take this opportunity to thank the many people who have helped make this book a reality. Everyone to whom I turned for help was right there with whatever it was I needed. Unfortunately, some will be left out. These were folks who I questioned in passing at car shows whose names I failed to get. People who allowed me to take pictures of their cars but failed to tell me the owners' names. To them as a group and as individuals I extend a very warm thank you!

Warm thanks go to those whose names I do know. First, to my brother Al Taylor who always stopped his work to help or answer any questions I had, even while in the middle of moving his entire shop! Next, very special thanks go to Chad Heath of Eagle One Products and Mike Pennington at Meguiar's. Both of these men gave me days of their time. Without their help, there would have been no book.

While working on the last two chapters I had the opportunity to meet George and Don Kordyak, who helped immeasurably by explaining all the details of starting your own business. The same thanks go to Sid and Kathy White, who have one of the most sophisticated detailing businesses I've had the pleasure of seeing.

Thanks go again to my long time friends Dave and Cindy Keetch. To Dave for his help in showing me what judging is all about and to Cindy for just being a good friend. Brother Al introduced me to Eric Rosenau, which let me make a new friend. Thank you, Eric, for your contribution both to this book and to the hobby.

John Pfanstiehl, of Pro Motorcar, also helped with material on paint finessing, color sanding and paint chip repair. His extra efforts have certainly added to the value of this book.

Bud Abraham, the owner of Detail Plus Systems in Portland, Oregon, deserves special thanks for providing information on the detailing business, which he consults for.

Over the years I've always been able to call on a friend who never failed to help. Jerry Olmsted, "The Birdman of Escondido," owns one of the West Coast's great Thunderbird restoration shops. Jerry has contributed to every book I've written. One more time, thanks, Jerry!

Another long time friend is Michael Lutfy, Editorial Director at HPBooks. Michael takes my very rough manuscripts and laboriously turns them into books that make sense to the reader. Thank you, Michael, for your efforts. And thanks for putting up with me!

Another dear soul who puts up with more than her share of automobiles and auto related activities is my dearest wife Ellen. Thank you for not throwing me out on my ear for tracking grease all over your living room carpet. Thanks also for over forty years of automobile related fun together!

ACKNOWLEDGMENTS

CONTENTS

Introduction   V

Chapter 1
DETAILING PRODUCTS & TOOLS1

Chapter 2
PROFESSIONAL HAND WASH   17

Chapter 3
PAINT INSPECTION &
EVALUATION   22

Chapter 4
PAINT CLEANING, POLISHING
& WAXING   33

Chapter 5
EXTERIOR DETAILS   50

Chapter 6
WHEELS & TIRES   65

Chapter 7
INTERIOR DETAILING   77

Chapter 8
ENGINE DETAILING   89

Chapter 9
Car Covers   102

Chapter 10
DETAILING AS
A BUSINESS   105

DETAILING FAQ'S   115

Someone, whose name has dimmed from the passage of time, once said, "Attention to detail is the key to success." I think it was his brother that said, "The Devil is in the details!" Both were right and a few moments' thought on the following example will tell you why.

Two perfect '57 Chevys are on display at a local Concours d'Elegance. The judges can't decide which is the most perfect car and should be declared class winner. Once again they carefully go over each car. Each is equally beautiful. The paint is perfect, the interiors are flawless and you could eat out of the engine compartment. It will come down to this: who has paid the closest attention to the details? Eventually, one of the judges will find a missing washer, a cad-plated bolt that should have been painted, or the sin of sins—a trail of oil, or a paint defect left from acid rain or an unlucky bird bomb. That speck of dirt, some brake dust on the inside of the wheel or a vinyl rear window with scratches is where you find the Devil. This book is dedicated to keeping the Devil at bay.

Detailing means far more than washing the car with dish soap and the kitchen sponge, then applying some paste wax and elbow grease. While fine for regular car care, it's not the reason you purchased this book. Detailing is not only a matter of technique and knowing what products to use, it is also a state of mind. It's what drives you to achieve a flawless paint, a rich, deep, glossy "wet" look, and you have to care about keeping it that way. Detailing means learning what man-made and natural environmental contaminants are hazardous to your paint, and taking steps to remove or protect your car from them.

In practice, auto detailing is the process of paying attention to all of the details on your car, from paint care, to upholstery, trim, stainless, the correct decals, plastic and window glass. It's a process that's really never done. It can always be a little bit better.

A good portion of this book is dedicated to the care and restoration of the painted exterior surface of your car. Although paint is by no means the only area that needs to be detailed, it is the largest and therefore will receive the most attention.

FIVE-STEP PROCESS

There is a widely prescribed five-step process that most detailers follow when it comes to the care and maintenance of your car's exterior paint. They are:

Washing—Removing the loose contaminants sitting on top of your paint finish.

Cleaning—Prepping the finish by removing oxidation, stains, blemishes and bonded contaminants.

Polishing—Creating high gloss/high reflection.

Protecting—Creating a barrier coat on top of the finish to protect the paint finish from the elements.

Maintaining—Keeping the finish looking like it was just polished...every day!

Depending on the condition of your painted surface, you may or may not need to follow all of these steps each time you take towel to car. But one thing is certain, if you regularly maintain a restored finish, it will remain so for a long period of time.

My one caution is: if I say test a product on an inconspicuous spot, please do so! Although manufacturers make every effort to test their products against the widest possible number of materials, they can't get to them all. Find a piece of the material, such as underneath the seat or dash, or for paint, on a door jamb or rocker panel, and test rub the product to make sure it doesn't dissolve paint or discolor the fabric or material. Enamel paint thinner is about the mildest solvent

there is—until you begin working with solvents for polyurethane enamels. These can dissolve just about anything. A cleaner for mag wheels may stain aluminum wheels. So please test products before applying them all over.

Throughout the book you will see many different products being used. Most of these products are available at your local auto parts store, and if they don't have it in stock, they can probably order it.

At the end of this book, I've added a section on how to set up your own detail business. This is a great way to make a good living with little investment and totally be your own boss. You'll learn what it takes to get into this business, what the cost of equipment will be, how to do the work and how to find customers.

You'll also learn what to charge, how to deal with problems, what licenses you need and just about everything it takes to set up the business but the soap. I've even interviewed several people in the business to tell you how they became successful.

Show enthusiast, car seller, detail shop owner or owner want-to-be, you've selected the one book that brings it all to you.

A Word on Safety

Although I continually mention safety procedures throughout this book where appropriate, I do advise you to take general precautions, particularly when it comes to using a high speed buffer. The buffer can be a trap for hair, loose clothing, a necktie—I know of one girl who lost her scalp! So please wear protective goggles, tie your hair back or put it under a cap if it is long, and secure loose garments.

I also strongly advise that when working under your car, make sure it is resting securely on jackstands. The hydraulic jack is not enough support. And finally, although I offer general directions for the use of some products, these may be different from the product you choose to use. Please make sure you read the labels of the products you are using, and if the directions are different than mine, follow them instead.

DETAILING

PRODUCTS

& TOOLS

Meguiar's has come a long way since 1906 when these 6 products were their stock-in-trade.

There are a wide variety of tools and products available for detailing. Walk into an auto parts store, and there are endless brands of waxes, sealers, polishes, finish restorers, glazes, cleaners, etc. What follows are suggestions of the tools you will need for serious detailing, and a rundown on the types of products available. This information should help you decide which type to buy.

DETAILING TOOLS

There are a number of tools that you'll find necessary, and others just helpful. Detailing has come a long way from a bucket, dish washing soap, a sponge, an old bathroom towel, and a can of paste wax. In this section, we'll go over most of the many tools available to the detailer today.

Buckets

You'll need two buckets rather than just one. One is for car wash solution, the other a rinse bucket. As you wash the car, you'll dip into the cleaning solution, wash an area, then rinse the wash mitt in the clear, clean water. This way, you do not carry dirty washing water—and the scratchy sand contained therein—to the surface of the paint.

Wash Mitt

Forget the sponge! Get a wash mitt. These come in wool or terrycloth. Each works equally well with the single exception that wool will carry more cleaning solution. The advantage of the mitt over a towel is its ability to hold lots of cleaning solution. Using lots of solution helps carry away the dirt with less chance of scratching the paint. The mitt is a very useful tool.

1

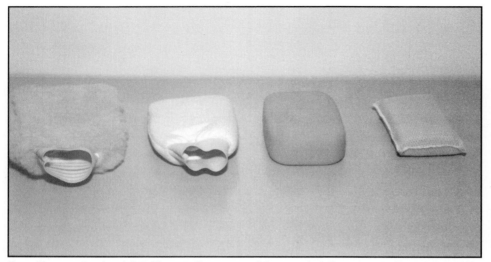

To achieve professional detailing results, you need to use what the pros use. From left to right is a lambs-wool mitt, terrycloth mitt, regular sponge and a "bug sponge," which has polypropylene webbing around it for light scouring action.

Using a chamois to dry your car is perhaps the best method to prevent water spotting and streaking. This is the ultimate natural chamois—pure goatskin. Although very efficient, a natural chamois is relatively expensive and does wear out.

Sponges

If you don't have a mitt, natural sponges are among the best items for washing cars. Although they cost more than synthetic sponges, they last much longer. The bigger the sponge, the better, because it will hold more soap and water and thereby allow you to cover more area before returning to the wash bucket. One sponge you'll need is a "bug sponge." This is a small sponge, about the size of a kitchen sponge. Around it is wrapped plastic netting. This slightly abrasive (but non-scratchy) material will quickly wash away even the driest dead bug. Whatever you do, don't use the type of kitchen sponge which has a rough pad on one side. It is too easy to make a mistake during washing and accidentally use the wrong side. This surface can really scratch. It can even permanently scuff the chrome finish on bumpers or trim parts.

Chamois

There are two types of chamois: natural and man-made. The natural chamois will absorb great quantities of water—more so than the man-made. A natural chamois is a piece of suede like leather oiled and tanned to make it soft and pliant. Once it has been wetted down and wrung out, it will soak up water like a sponge, but will leave the surface dry and streak-free. Plus, unlike a towel or cloth, it won't leave behind lint clinging to the paint. After a few uses, though, the natural chamois begins to get stiff as the oils are washed out. Fortunately, this stiffness goes away when the chamois is wet. However, the stiffness, when dry, makes the chamois hard to store. It's like a big board. The disadvantage of the natural chamois, compared to the man-made, is its shorter life and high cost. A less expensive alternative is the synthetic chamois. Some of the synthetic

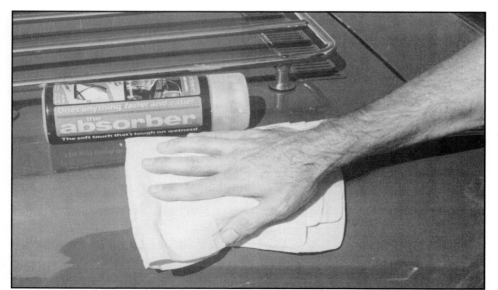

Many detailers use a synthetic chamois. The synthetic costs less, absorbs up to 50% more water, lasts longer and can be rolled up and conveniently stored in the bottle shown here. Photo by John Pfanstiehl.

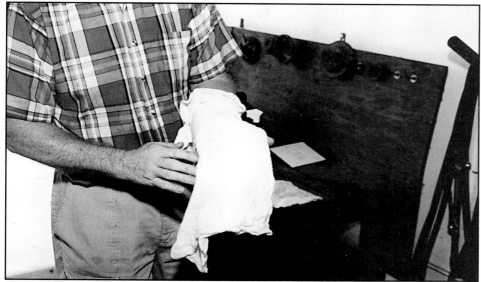

You'll need more towels than just about anything else. When it comes to towel material, there's little that compares with cotton terrycloth. If you can find them in this age of Huggies™, cotton diapers are a good substitute for removing polish and wax. Stay away from T-shirts, especially those with silk screened or embroidered artwork.

chamois work remarkably well and often hold up better than the natural variety. Plus they cost about a third as much. The Absorber™ is a particular brand that picks up more water than a natural chamois and it stores away wet, which you'll find is another advantage.

Dry Cleaning Cloths—Dry clean your car? Well, almost. A type of cloth called a dry cleaning cloth has been available for years. These are soft cloths treated with a cleaner to help remove light films and dirt from cars. They are used by some car dealers who find it easier to just wipe down the dust which accumulates on the cars overnight instead of doing a complete wash to every car on the lot. Although dry wash cloths shouldn't be used on heavily soiled cars, they certainly are much faster and easier for a quick, light cleaning. If there is any grit on the car, it may scratch the finish. If you have a dark-colored car or if you're very picky about its finish, be cautious when wiping down your car with a dry cleaning cloth.

Towels

You need a minimum of two separate groups of towels. One group will be used with products containing silicone, the other must never be contaminated with chemical. Silicone on the windshield is nearly impossible to get off and it leaves a smeared surface. If you plan to do any painting, you'll not want silicone anywhere near your surface. Silicone is the main reason for "birdseyes" in new paint. So, keep two sets of towels; you may want to keep even more. The professionals keep them separated by color. White for non-silicone products and black for products containing this wonderful, but difficult to deal with, chemical product.

If you polish and wax by hand, you may want to keep separate sets for application and buffing of each product. Buffing (rubbing) compounds are more abrasive than polishing compounds. If you should try polishing with a towel that still has compound on it, you run the risk of scratching the surface you're polishing. Likewise, if you have polish on your waxing towel, you risk the same problem. I suggest you have a different color towel for each application, including window washing, interior cleaning, etc.

Brushes

There are brushes of every size and description for every job. There are

Here are but a few of the many brushes available to the detailer. From left to right is a feather duster, a soft brush for delicate material, a stiff scrub brush that could be used for carpet care, a detailer's "toothbrush" (available with plastic, brass, and stainless steel bristles). Next to it is a brush for wire wheels and my favorite, the cut-off paint brush.

These handy swipes from Eagle One are shaped to a tire's sidewall to evenly apply tire dressing and prevent sags and runs. Courtesy Eagle One

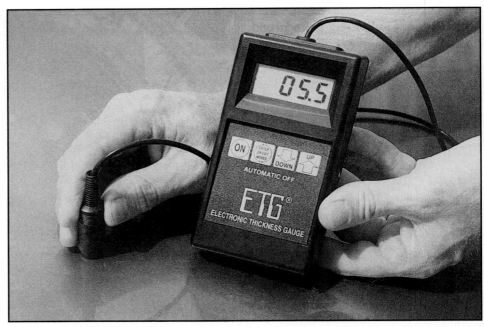

To really determine if you will have enough paint to finesse out defects, you'll need a paint thickness gauge. These devices, available from Pro Motorcar Products at 813/726-9225, will tell you how many mils of paint are in and around a particular defect, be it a scratch or chemical spot. Courtesy Pro Motorcar.

acid swabs, brushes for cleaning carpet, for upholstery, tires, wheels, spoke wheels and excessive dirt on the body. My favorite brush is a 2-inch nylon paint brush with the bristles cut off about halfway down. This gives a very stiff but gentle brush. It's great for removing dried wax around chrome, brushing crumbs out of the area under the seat-cover welt, getting into grooves, nooks and crannies for washing, or just brushing. Two or three of these brushes will take the place of much of the vast array of those on the market.

I like to keep a selection of brushes that look much like toothbrushes but have bristles of stiff plastic, brass and stainless steel. These are great for rust removal, hardened grease and other problem areas. They are available, three to a package, one each of plastic, brass and stainless steel bristles. (Apply a little Flitz polish to the brass brush to get the rust you'll find between the bumper and bumper guard on autos where these items were chrome plated.)

Although it's not really a brush, I'll add it here anyway. Buy a small feather duster for the interior. You'll find lots of uses for it there.

Squeegee

This is a maybe yes or maybe no product. If you're a professional, or plan to become one, it will make window cleaning go faster. If you're just doing the family car it won't do much for you except maybe leave streaks on the window. Using your chamois is more effective.

Vacuum Cleaner and Attachments

If you're going to buy a vacuum cleaner, buy the most powerful shop vac you can afford. At this writing, Sears offers a shop vac that includes a separate blower. This is great for blowing water out of areas like the groove between the fender and the body, around the door jambs and other areas where water likes to hide.

The most important attachment for your vacuum is the long narrow wand designated as the tool for cleaning venetian blinds. This tool really gets down into the cracks and grooves, especially between the seat and the side-body rail. The second most important is the brush. I like this tool for cleaning the instrument panel. It's also a must for vacuuming headliners.

Professional Tools

These are tools that may not be necessary, but are sure helpful if you can afford them.

Temperature Gauge—Professionals like to know the temperature of the paint. If the surface of the paint is too hot, chemicals for working it will not react as they should. Buffing compounds dry too quickly, waxes also dry too fast and streak. By knowing the surface temperature the professional knows how his or her chemicals will work

Paint Thickness Gauges—This

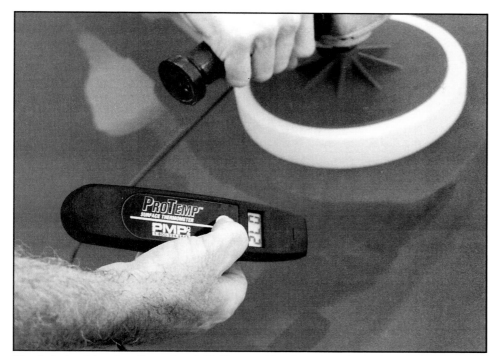

Worried about burning through paint? The combination above is designed to reduce the likelihood of such a catastrophe. The Black & Decker buffer has electronic speed control to prevent the speed from rapidly increasing when pressure is removed from the wheel. Meguiar's foam pads are more forgiving than wool pads and therefore also reduce the chances of burning the paint. The latest advance is the use of Pro Temp non-contact thermometers to check the surface temperature of the paint while learning buffing or while testing out new polishes, pads, or paints. Temperature build-up during buffing is particularly critical on fiberglass or composite panels because they don't absorb or dissipate heat as well as steel or aluminum panels. Courtesy Pro Motorcar Products

The QFM instrument is a relatively affordable instrument which can measure the quality of a paint's surface finish. The battery powered QFM enables painters, dealerships, detailers and manufacturers to set and monitor the quality of the finish on cars, match repaint to factory finishes, or show the quality of work to customers. It's available from Pro Motorcar Products at 813/726-9225.

can determine just how much buffing the clear coat can take before it becomes buffed through. There are expensive digital electronic versions, but you can also get by with a less expensive magnetic gauge. More on how to take thickness readings is on page 29.

Glossmeter—Pro Motorcar has developed a nifty new device that measures "Distinctness of Image—Gloss." The instrument, called a Quality of Finish Measurement instrument (QFM) is a small, handheld battery powered instrument that enables measurement and evaluation of automotive finishes. For more details, see Chapter 3, page 32.

Loupe—A loupe is a photographer's tool. The photographer uses it to inspect his or her proof sheet or transparencies for sharpness, detail in the shadows and overall appearance. The detailer can use it to view flaws in the paint. Is that a chip or a bug? Is the ring I see sitting on top of the paint or is it etched into it? How deep is that scratch? This is a great tool.

Paint Cleaning Tools

When the car has been thoroughly washed, it may need to be "cleaned." This means removing surface defects such as oxidation and acid rain spots. These techniques are covered in Chapter 4. However, there are several tools associated with this effort.

Ultrafine Sandpaper—Detailing companies such as Meguiar's and 3M offer microfine sandpaper grits for colorsanding and for removing surface scratches. Get an assortment of grits from 600 to 2000. For more details, see the sidebar nearby.

Variable Speed Rotary Buffer—Pneumatic or electric, the purpose of the buffer/polisher is to rotate at a

great tool measures the thickness of the paint. With just a little arithmetic the user can determine how thick the clear coat is. Knowing this, the user

TRUE GRITS

by John Pfanstiehl, Pro Motorcar, Inc.

Abrasives have changed to meet the demands of the new paint systems. Bud Abraham of Detail Plus is now offering a Cera finishing paper which is a super fine emery paper graded in 8,000 and 10,000 grit. Detail Plus also offers a new sanding solution Clay Plus which comes in an 8 oz brick. Applied with water, one of its benefits is the reduction in use of solvents making it an environmentally friendly new product. Bud also recommends that paint shops beware of the ingredients in off-the-shelf waxes and detail shop products because many contain silicones.

3M has introduced fine grades of finishing film discs for use on DA's to help productivity in the shop. Their Stikit P 1200 paper for example can be used dry to remove orange peel and thereby eliminate the need for the clean up and drying associated with wet sanding. In their Perfect-It system, the sanding would be followed by rubbing compound. The final step would usually be application of their Machine Glaze, which comes in Light and Dark for lighter or darker color cars. 3M cautions to "Always use the least aggressive procedure that will effectively do the job."

Finishing papers have also become color-coded. The Lapika brand of papers from Eagle are available in grits ranging from their L-400 to L-1500. Eagle states that their "roller coating system" used to produce the Lapika papers results in a more uniform grit which reduces the depth of scratches during use.

For finessing minor defects, and for color sanding, you'll need ultrafine sandpaper, ranging in grits from 600 to 2000 grit (shown above). These are more like "polishing" papers than sandpaper.

The orbital polisher is often mistakenly called a buffer, which refers to removing top layers of paint to restore gloss. The orbital is good for applying and removing wax, however, and its orbital action prevents it from burning paint.

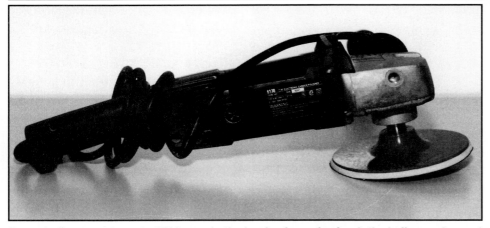

Power buffers operate up to 4500 rpm. In the hands of a professional, the buffer can be used effectively to restore paint to a deep gloss, using the right chemicals, of course. But in the hands of a less experienced person, it can melt clear coat and paint right through to the metal in the blink of an eye. Practice on scrap metal, burning through the paint on purpose to get a feel for how quickly it can happen.

high speed, usually from 1800 to 4500 rpm, which creates friction and heat, thereby softening the paint. Once the paint is softened, you can either correct the surface irregularity and/or create a high shine using the appropriate pad and chemical. Most paint finish problems require the use of a high speed buffer. Even clear coats with severe etching or scratches will require the use of a buffer to correct the problem. Some models come with true variable speeds, controlled by a trigger, while most offer one, two or three different speeds selected with a switch. Using this machine requires considerable practice before committing it to actually rubbing out the paint on your car. It's very, very easy to burn right through your paint and into the primer! Never use a high speed buffer

Meguiar's has a color-coded system to label their pads, and others have similar systems. From left to right is a wool bonnet for aggressive buffing, a red polyfoam cutting pad (less aggressive than the wool pad) used on the orbital buffer, the yellow pad for polishing, tan for finishing and the small yellow again for polishing but used on a small orbital polisher.

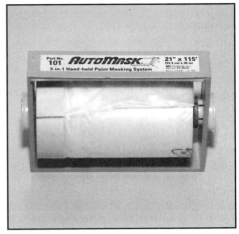

Masking tape should be used to cover door, hood and trunk edges where the paint is especially thin to prevent burning through it. You may also want to cover certain panels with a sheet of plastic or "visqueen," as shown above, to protect paint from any caustic chemicals you may use, such as engine degreaser.

on paint less than 3 mils thick.

Orbital Polishers—Technically speaking, orbital buffers can not be called a buffer or a polisher, since it does not revolve in a rotating motion that creates the friction and heat generated by a rotary tool. In actuality, the orbital duplicates the hand motion that would apply and remove wax or sealant. With some good finishes, it is possible as a first step to chemically clean the finish with an orbital and then apply the wax or sealant. Which you do depends on the paint finish. The orbital is becoming an essential tool for detailing, especially with clear coat finishes that often do not require the use of a high speed buffer for minor polishing defects. Orbitals are available as either electric or pneumatic. There is also a mini pneumatic orbital waxer that weighs less than three pounds.

Pads/Bonnets—Pads are generally used with the rotary buffer/polishers and bonnets with the orbital tools. Pads can be grouped into two categories: cutting and finishing pads. Cutting pads are woven wool and available in diameters of 7" to 9" with and without the new Velcro attachment and lengths of 3/4" to 1-1/2". The purpose is to remove the paint surface irregularity: orange peel, surface scratches, water spots, etc. Without exception, the cutting pad will cause swirls in the paint when used with an abrasive compound. That is why you must follow its use with a finishing pad. Buffing pads are color coded for their level of cutting action. The "red" pad, which is more burgundy in color, is designed for heavy cutting action and is somewhat akin to the cutting action of the least aggressive wool pad. Use this with light rubbing compounds.

The yellow pad is less aggressive than the red pad and is considered a polishing pad. It has a very light cutting action. Use it for applying polish during that stage of your exterior detailing. One of the primary advantages of both the red and yellow pads is that neither produces swirl marks.

The tan pad is considered to be a finishing pad and is used for very light polishing or wax application. It has no cutting action.

Finishing pads fall into three types: 100% sheepskin; sheepskin/synthetic mix; and foam. The 100% sheepskin pads have been the standard for detailers wanting a show car finish. The drawback is the price. By far the most popular is the sheepskin-synthetic mix to polish and remove swirls. Reason: less expensive price.

With the clear coat finishes, the foam polishing pad has become quite popular with detailers. It leaves no swirls, or removes swirls; it requires no maintenance to speak of, but it does not last more than 5-6 cars.

Bonnets, as mentioned, are used with the orbital waxer. They are

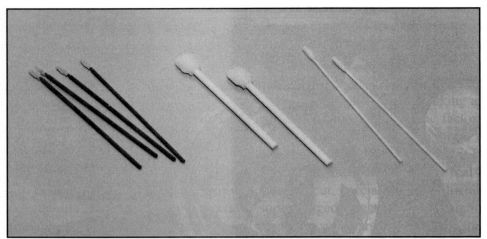

These are special detailing cotton swabs, used to get into crevices and areas your finger can't. They are pretty trick, but you can achieve similar results with a toothpick or shish kabob skewer wrapped in cotton.

broken medallions to the body while the cement dries.

Cotton-Tipped Applicators

These rascals are the backbone of the industry and are synonymous with the word "detailing." In my photo illustrations you can see they now come in every size, shape and length you could want. Use them to clean in the very tightest of places. You can also make your own by wrapping cotton around toothpicks.

DETAILING PRODUCTS

The type and variety of products available to the detailer is mind-boggling. But remember, they are grouped generally into the categories of washing, cleaning, polishing and protecting.

Washing Products

The following products are designed for washing, to get the items

usually made of terry cloth and provide sufficient abrasiveness to easily remove cleaner, polish, wax or sealants. Normally, two are used per chemical application, one to apply it, a second to remove it.

A new innovation in orbital bonnet technology is the se of 100% sheepskin or sheepskin/synthetic mix. These bonnets are only used to remove lighter waxes and sealants to provide a scratch-free finish on dark cars.

New pads are also making their appearance. Foam pads are less aggressive than wool pads and are now commonly used for the final polishing and for removal of swirl marks. And now there are even different grades of foam pads, color-coded so that it's easier to remember which pad to use with which polish. New varieties of wool pads are also available and for large volume or production shops, Schlegel, a leading pad manufacturer, says that wool pads are the fastest solution to dirt in a paint job. New finer wool polishing pads are also coming out which will reduce linting and fine scratches or swirl marks.

Masking Tape

There are two tapes you'll never find me without: masking tape and duct tape. Both are indispensable but masking tape helps do the job. Mask off any trim before you begin to buff to prevent burning it or otherwise damaging it. Likewise, place a strip along hood and trunk edges to protect them also. Use masking tape to hold

Today's dish soaps, long an amateur favorite, are formulated to cut grease, and will strip the wax on your car. There are a number of car wash soaps available, both professional and consumer, that have the proper formulations to protect paint.

SOAPS AND DETERGENTS
Courtesy P&S Sales

Chemically, soaps and detergents are fairly complex and diverse but the concept of how they work is very simple. In fact soaps are one of the oldest forms of chemistry, having been used for centuries.

Basic Soap

Soaps clean dirt and oil by surrounding the dirt and oil particles with soap molecules and allowing them to be dissolved in water.

Simple, eh? A soap molecule is made up of a long chain of atoms (between 10 and 40). One side of the molecule likes dirt and oil and the other side of the molecule likes water. When soap is mixed with dirt and oil then rinsed, the dirt liking side is attracted to the dirt and surrounds the particle. When you rinse away the soap, all the water liking tails stick out into the water and look like millions of microscopic spiny sea urchins.

Why Detergents?

Soap has a few problems, the biggest is that soap is badly affected by hard water. Chemists found that by using similarly shaped molecules (long molecules with dirt liking and water liking ends) they could get better cleaning and less problems with hard water.

These are called detergents. There were a few problems with early detergents also. Since they were designed to be such long lasting cleaners, natural processes could not break them down and they built up in the environment until they became a pollution problem. Now, most detergents still in use today are as biodegradable or more biodegradable than soaps.

basically clean.

Washing Liquids—Never use dish washing soap (detergent) to wash your car. Detergent is a natural wax stripper and the product used to strip wax from vinyl tile floors! You'll actually wash off your wax the first time you wash your car with detergent. Instead, buy one of the brand name cleaning solutions designed for auto exteriors. Meguiar's has two products called Car Wash & Conditioner (designed to be safe for paint with a clear coat) and Soft Wash Gel. Eagle One's product is called Car Wash & Wax Conditioner. This is one of the most important products for long term car care. If you send your car through the car wash, you can never be sure whether or not they are using detergent. Use these facilities at your own risk.

Bug And Tar Remover—Some manufacturers combine both products in one aerosol can, others treat each one individually. All of them seem to work well, especially the bug stuff. Remember, however, these products may strip the wax from your car, especially the tar remover.

Wax And Silicone Remover—Here is a product guaranteed to strip off your wax. That's what it was designed for. It, however, is the most powerful of the tar removing agents. If you have ever driven over a road that has just been reoiled, retarred or resurfaced, you'll understand how difficult it is to remove these products, especially after they've dried for a week or two. Wax and silicone remover will take it off. Buy this by the gallon at automotive paint stores.

Vinyl And Convertible Top Cleaning—Use your car washing liquid for both of these tops. If you happen to be washing the convertible

The thing to remember about wheel cleaners is to check to make sure it is compatible with the metal type of your wheel. Wheel cleaners are generally caustic chemicals designed to cut through and dissolve brake dust. Check to make sure that the wheel cleaner you choose is safe for your wheels. As shown, a different cleaner exists for chrome, mags and aluminum.

Leather requires special care, and there are special cleaners and conditioners. Do not use saddlesoap and neatsfoot oil for automotive leather. These products are not formulated for the leather used in automotive interiors.

You'll find a dizzying array of tire dressings, conditioners, cleaners, protectants, restorers, etc. What works best? Personal preference is more the rule of thumb. If the tire has a brown ring around it (called blooming) then you'll need to deep clean it. A one-step, spray on and walk away type of product may not be sufficient. Go with a cleaner, followed up with a dressing.

top of an Asian or European luxury car with a cloth top (Haartz Cloth or Cambic) be sure to rinse very, very well. If you have stubborn spots on a vinyl top, use one of the vinyl cleaners designed to clean vinyl interiors. Follow this with a vinyl conditioner or protectant.

Tires & Wheels—Tire and wheel care has spawned its own mini-industry. There are so many different materials from which the wheels are made, it became necessary to make a product for each wheel. Therefore, when you go shopping for a wheel cleaner, be sure to get one that is designed either as a general purpose cleaner or is specific to your wheel: paint, chrome, aluminum or magnesium.

Tires are a different matter. There are cleaners, dressings and protectants. Cleaners will be necessary if there is a brown ring, called blooming, around the tire. Westley's Bleche-Wite is the best product for cleaning whitewalls and white lettering. There are some spray on and walk away dressings that work well if the tire is relatively clean. Protectants and dressings usually have different levels of gloss. In general, you don't want too much of a shine to the point where the tire looks unnaturally bright.

Vinyl Cleaners—Again, many manufacturers try to incorporate a cleaner and conditioner into a one-step process for interior trim. However, single products devoted to one task seem to be more effective. Vinyl cleaning products can usually be sprayed onto the vinyl and scrubbed with a brush. A good trick for vinyl floor covers in trucks, which tend to get filthy, is to use tire cleaner.

Interior Protectants—There are a wide variety of vinyl protectants available, and they are not all the same. First, look for a water-based protectant. Some are solvent-based with potentially hazardous ingredients, such as petroleum distillates, alcohol and kerosene, and can emit fumes and shouldn't be used inside closed spaces, such as a garage. Second, look for a protectant with UV absorbers, the more strength the better.

Leather Cleaners And Conditioners—Use these products the same way you use vinyl products with the exception of spraying the cleaner onto the leather and scrubbing. This is far too harsh. Spray the cleaner onto a piece of toweling, gently clean the leather surface followed by gentle drying. Use a conditioner for leather as described for vinyl.

Carpet Shampoo—In general, a

Manufacturers of auto detailing products are focused on formulating a product to remove and clean stains and dirt common to cars only. That's one factor to consider when choosing a cleaner. To do a thorough, professional job, you really need a shampoo/vac machine, available for rent from supermarkets and hardware stores.

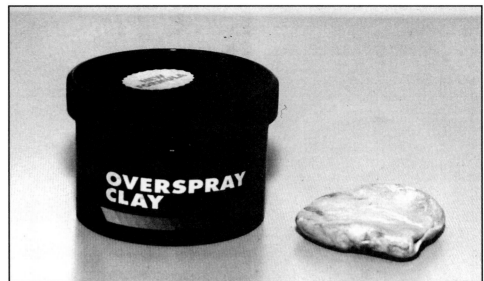

Detailing clay is sold under many brand names, but the purpose is the same: to remove minor paint defects and particles caused by industrial fallout, such as smog, acid rain, and iron particles.

carpet shampoo formulated for the specific type of grease and oil stains that will be found on a floor mat are probably going to work better than a catchall type of carpet shampoo for the household. Most consumer oriented detail product manufacturers make a carpet shampoo. I've personally had good success with several household products, including "Gonzo" which is sometimes hard to find. Call The Gonzo Corporation at (617) 828-7779 in Canton, MA for the location of your nearest supplier. The other product is called "Resolve" and will be found in the soaps and cleaners section of your local supermarket. These two products do

an excellent job of stain removal.

Clear Plastic Cleaners—Both Eagle One and Meguiar's manufacture a plastic cleaner and polish. These are great for the clear vinyl curtain in convertible tops, for the face of instrument clusters and any other clear vinyl or plastic (taillight lenses, medallions, etc.).

Window Cleaners—If your car has tinted windows, I strongly suggest you use a window cleaning product designed specifically for this. Household window cleaner can etch this vinyl film, reducing your visibility.

Exterior Paint Cleaning Products

These are the items that can be most confusing, but essentially, they are products designed to remove mild surface defects, oxidation and to prepare the surface for polishing. Cleaning products are what we call rubbing or buffing compounds. Not every car will need to be "rubbed out" or cleaned to this extent. Chapter 2

will tell you how to judge the condition of your paint to determine what it needs. If the paint has heavy oxidation, then heavy compounding is called for. If your paint is in excellent condition, you can skip the cleaning step and go right to polishing.

Always start with the least aggressive compound you think might do the job. If it doesn't give you the results you want, switch to a more aggressive product. By using the least aggressive material possible, you extend the life of you paint. Remember, in this step you are actually removing either color or clearcoat. Take it easy!

Detailing Clay—The ultimate in washing your car is the use of detailing clay, or as it's often called, fallout clay. This product is used either during the washing process, or afterward with a lubricant. As you can see in the chapter on washing, this product looks like a patty of plasticine clay or Silly Putty. It is formed into the shape of a hamburger, then lubricated with suds and wiped over

The Collector's Choice classic car care system, available from TrimParts 513/831-1472, is a favorite among car enthusiasts.

Paint cleaning products vary in their degree of abrasiveness. You'll want to start with the least abrasive cleaner first. If it doesn't work, then go heavier. But keep in mind these abrasives remove paint, and the idea is to obviously remove as little as possible.

the surface area with minor defects. It removes fallout from acid rain, bug droppings, jet fuel, and the corrosion from iron particles mixed with acid rain that causes corrosive damage to the surface of the paint. It also removes hard water spots in some cases. It does not, however, remove the wax!

Compounds—Rubbing compounds, as they have traditionally been called, come in soft pastes or liquids and include a variety of different types of hard to soft abrasives which might include silica, diatomaceous earth or even talc, depending on what the formulator is attempting to achieve with the product. In general, compounds fall into three categories: heavy, medium or light. In addition to the abrasive they include solvents and oils, in varying degrees, and a number of secondary elements. Their purpose, used in conjunction with a high-speed buffer and cutting pad, is to correct a

paint surface irregularity. Obviously, the heavy-duty compound is used for severe oxidation, scratches, etching or orange peel. You should never use a heavy-duty compound on a clear coat finish. The light-duty compound differs from the other mentioned compounds in terms of the type of abrasive used in the product. It has abrasive, however light, but it is in the product.

However you try to shake it out, a light-duty compound can provide for your operation a product that will offer "chemical" cleaning of a good surface that is stained; elimination of light surface scratches and water spots and finally a product you can use on scratched or spotted clear coat finishes. If you have a product that can do all this why would you need one especially for clear coats? Think about it.

The formulation we use has an extra amount of mineral oil to keep the

product "wet." That is, it does not dry quickly when used with a high-speed buffer and this helps to prevent burning. It also reduces the amount of product needed to buff the surface.

Combination Products—In an effort to make life easier, many manufacturers have made combination products. These are usually compounds that clean and wax at the same time and are called cleaner-waxes. Their purpose is to provide a quick one-step cleaning and shining of the painted surface. They can be used with a high-speed buffer and finishing pad or applied with an orbital. If a cleaner glaze/one-step product is used, nothing more should be done to the vehicle. If the finish is unsatisfactory after its use, then you have used the wrong product or applied it with the wrong tool and pad. The cleaner glaze product was primarily designed again for the auto dealer car where all that was needed was a quick high shine. (Given the finish was in good enough condition to justify only a one-step product.)

They can also be used for detailing cars where you sell a simple wash and

POLYMERS, RESINS & SILICONE
Courtesy P& S Sales

Many labels on wax products contain the word "polymer" to hype the product. It would therefore be helpful to know exactly what this means.

Polymers

The simplest definition for polymer is also the most descriptive: "poly" means many and "mer" means unit. So, any chemical that consists of endlessly repeating identical chemical units is a polymer. Polymers include such (now familiar yet somewhat incomprehensible) materials as polyethylene, polyurethane, polytetrafluoroethylene (PTFE) and polyisocyanate. Notice how the chemical name always starts with "poly" followed by another word. For example, poly-ethylene is many units of ethylene. Polymers also include more familiar materials such as wood, starch, rubber, protein and DNA. As can be seen from the latter list, polymers can have an endless variety of properties. In the car polish industry, the word polymer is the single most abused term I can think of.

For example, most of the thickeners used in car polishes and waxes are polymers, which makes it suspiciously easy to put the words "contains polymer" on the bottle. Judge your product by how it works for you, not because the word polymer is on the label.

That being said, there are polymers that can make large improvements in the quality of automobile finish products. But they have to meet certain criteria to make them better than waxes or silicone fluids. The most important criteria is a chemical reaction called "cross linking," which means that there has to be a way for each one of these long chain polymers to connect together. If a polymer crosslinks, it can form a durable net of polymer over the surface of the paint. Depending on other properties of the polymer and the cross link, a more durable coating can be formed than could otherwise be achieved without the polymer.

Silicone

Silicone fluid is a relatively short chain inorganic polymer called polydimethyl siloxane; please note the prefix poly before the units of dimethyl siloxane. The chain is not long enough to be typically called a polymer but by the technical definition, it is a polymer. Again we see here, the name "polymer" means less and less every time you see it. The properties of silicone fluids range from very thin, volatile liquids that look and feel like petroleum solvents to thick heavy liquids that look like crystal clear honey. The only difference between the thin liquid and the honey liquid is the number of units in the dimethylsiloxane chain.

Resins

The chemical dictionary states that the term resin is "so broadly used as to be almost meaningless." Resin is a catch all term. But, usually, a resin is a polymer that melts or is soluble in specific solvents. In some cases the base material used to make a plastic is called a resin where the finished product containing plasticizers and fillers is called plastic. So, how do you know what resin is being referred to on a product label? You don't. What does resin do for a polish or sealant? Since there are so many materials that can be classified as a resin, it is anybody's guess. As with most of the complex sounding names on labels, they are marketing jargon. Use the product that provides the performance and characteristics that you like, not because there is a long name on the label.

---

wax; express detail; "hand wax" or other such low cost services. Remember, if you use a cleaner glaze, by definition, it is not necessary to wash or seal the finish afterwards.

Exterior Polishes

We come now to the third of our five step process. The car is washed and cleaned and now it must be polished. By a polish I mean a product that is used as the next step after the compound to remove swirls and polish the paint. It would also be used as a first step on a good paint

Classic cars have yards of chrome, and need a special polish. After polishing, you can add a light coat of wax to the chrome for added protection.

Exterior details must be taken care of to complete the detailing job. This means special products and attention for glass, plastic and black trim. There are products available for all of these items from many different manufacturers.

finish to create a high shine. A "good" polish would include light abrasives to remove swirls, oils, solvents and silicones for ease of use. To remove swirls a polish must be used with a high-speed buffer and finishing pad. If you use an orbital to remove swirls, at best you will only fill them and after three or four car washes they will show as the filler washes away. On a particularly good finish, especially a clear coat, you could use the polish with an orbital as a first step to clean and polish the surface before wax or sealant application.

Chrome Polish—Every major manufacturer of auto cleaning compounds also makes a chrome polish. All are designed to be hand applied. You place a small dab on

your towel and rub it onto the chrome, using more product and more effort where rust spots have developed. When the polish is dry then wipe it off. The product I like best is called Flitz and is available in most parts houses and paint stores. This German product does an exceptional job on all metals and never scratches.

Wheel Polishes—Again, as with wheel cleaners, we enter a very specialized realm. There are polishes for each type of wheel as well as cleaner/polishes and polish/wax combinations. Here, you must again do a little experimenting on your own to find just the product you like. All are good, but as is often the case, you'll find one product that does just the job you want, where that same product might not do the best job for me. It just seems to work that way. When everything is polished out, you must protect the finish.

Waxes

Everything you've done so far has been to create the best shine possible for your paint. Now, this shine must be protected. Waxes are available in pastes, creams or liquids; they can contain natural or synthetic waxes; by name: carnauba, paraffin, synthetic carnauba. They will also contain oils, solvents and silicones. Their purpose is to provide protection and enhance the shine left by the polish. There is really no major difference between pastes, creams or liquids other than the amount of water or solvent in the formulation. The more water the softer the product; the less water and more solvent the harder the product.

Carnauba Wax—In its purest form, it is the most durable and most protective type of wax. Carnauba wax is a resin produced by the wax palm tree Copernicia cerifera. This tree grows in various parts of South America, but the trees in Northeastern

BEWARE THE "MAGIC POTION!"

When a product sounds too good to be true, it is too good to be true. In recent years, we have been bombarded with all types of protection products that promise year long, multi-year and sometimes lifetime protection. And while we would all like to have a product that would keep our cars looking like new for a year or more with just one application, it is simply not possible. Think of all the paint protection products that have come and gone over the last few years that at first sounded like they were the final solution to our car care problems. Each one filled the airwaves and store shelves for a year or two and then disappeared because no one would buy a second bottle. Some even light hoods on fire to supposedly prove miraculous durability. But the truth is that the hood in such demonstrations barely gets warm because heat rises. It's an old trick that is a demonstration of physics, not paint protection. Unfortunately, the disappointment and frustration that comes from believing the hype and using these products is causing more and more people to become less excited about waxing their own cars at all. There are few things more frustrating than spending several hours waxing your car only to end up with disappointing results. As bad as that is, the real problem comes when the promise of a year or multi-year protection is believed. A car's paint finish left unattended, except for washing, for a year or more will begin to take on the texture of sandpaper. At that point, getting the finish back to being as smooth as glass becomes a big job.

Sealants—The term "sealant" seems to have different meanings for different groups. Detail people expect their sealant products to have extra durability, forming a protective film over the paint. Whereas body shops and automobile painters call a product a sealant if 1) they can not repaint the area after using the product or 2) it will impair the solvent evaporation from a newly painted surface. Lastly, paint manufacturers call a product a sealant if the product will stop "bleed through" of undesirable properties from lower layers of paint or substrate to the newly painted surface, such as a primer.

This has created a lot of confusion over the past years. The consumer has to recognize the point of view of the person to whom they are talking to understand which type of sealant is being referred to. For a detailer, a sealant product should be one that forms some sort of cross linking film over the surface of the paint, forming a durable barrier on the surface. Such as a polymer like amino functional silicones. Just beware of the other terminologies that easily confuse the discussion.

Maintenance Products

You've done a ton of work getting your car this far. Now you must maintain it. Very little work is required. Wash it regularly with a washing solution as discussed earlier. Use detail clay to keep off the elements, then use one of the many products that help keep the shine up.

Meguiar's has a product called "Quick Detailer Mist & Wipe." Spray on and wipe off every other day or so, and you'll extend the time between polishing and waxing. You can possibly wipe down your car every

tropical rain forests of Brazil are thought to produce some of the highest quality. Carnauba is available in various grades of purity and clarity: #1 yellow is the top grade going downward to #2 yellow, #3 yellow, and various other commercial grades. Carnauba has a very strong grain structure and is the hardest wax known to man. In addition to being incredibly durable, carnauba dries to a deep, natural shine (in contrast, bees wax, paraffin and many synthetic waxes tend to cloud and occlude).

Teflon™ Waxes—Teflon is a trademark name of DuPont Chemicals for a polymer (see sidebar) known as polytetrafluoroethylene, aka PTFE. Teflon is an example of a polymer that is not well suited for use in a car wax because of several other

properties unrelated to its durable slippery nature. Teflon is a powder that melts at 600°F or dissolves in fluorinated solvents such as freon. Those are the only known ways to make Teflon into a liquid form. This is the main reason that Teflon is poorly suited for car wax. If it can't be made into a liquid, it can't be made into a coating. If it won't coat the surface, it won't stay there. Teflon is a powder that gets wiped away with the other powders in a wax or polish.

Eagle One claims to have had success with a low temperature bonding Teflon, and backs up their Teflon wax with a guaranty. I find it hard to tell the difference between a car waxed with Teflon and one waxed with carnauba. I'm still from the old school and use carnauba paste wax.

For maintenance, try one of the wipe on, wipe off quick detailing products available. These products are designed to remove very light dust and fallout from a finish that is already waxed and polished. Simply spray on, wipe off and walk away. Using these products will extend the life of each polishing and waxing job.

Detailing is big business! There are a mind-boggling number of products available to you as a consumer and as a professional. Some products make wild claims about their ability to protect and restore paint finishes. You can eliminate a lot of trial and error by sticking to the basics, and by choosing a product suited for a particular application. A good rule of thumb to follow is that if a product seems too good to be true, it probably is. Courtesy Pro Motorcar Products.

day, spray a little onto your towel, wipe it on gently then wipe it dry. It only takes a few minutes and helps keep that shine going between waxings.

Eagle One also has an excellent product called "5 Minute Detailer." It's applied in the same way and keeps your car really looking great.

There are lots of other products on the market that do the same job. Try several until you find the one that works best for your paint. Remember, every paint job is different and will react differently to each product.

Engine Degreasers

The engine presents its own challenges, but mainly, there are several things to mention about degreasers.

Water Soluble Degreasers—These are the degreasers you'll find in most of the parts stores. Names that come to mind are "Gunk" and "Berryman's." I believe that Gunk is probably one of the oldest degreasers on the market. I remember using it in the '50's.

The best way to use a degreaser is with the family's one or two gallon pressure sprayer, usually reserved for spraying roses with insecticide. Buy a gallon of degreaser, load it into the sprayer and spray the engine. Follow the directions on the container as some products work best with the engine cold while others perform better with the engine hot.

WD-40—The second degreaser, and my favorite, is WD-40. Just spray it on and rinse it off. It works every bit as well as a water-soluble degreaser and leaves no smell when you're done. I think you'll like the convenience of this degreasing operation. Want to know more? See Chapter 8.

For a proper, professional hand wash, you need the proper equipment: mitts instead of rags, at least two buckets, and car wash liquid. You'll also need bug and tar remover, a good hose with high pressure nozzle, and your chamois. The dual bucket above has one receptacle for rinsing, one for sudsing. The tray, which holds the products, fits inside when empty, all closing up into one neat container. Photo by John Pfanstiehl

Many professional detailers will work from the inside out to allow time for the carpet to dry as they polish and wax the car. But we're going to work from the outside in, on the surface most people care about—the paint surface. But in order to accurately evaluate the the paint, you must wash it thoroughly. I visited both Eagle One and Meguiar's, who both bent over backwards to help me in any way possible. What follows is a combination of instructions direct from the folks who are some of the best in the business.

PREPARATION

The first step is to assemble your washing kit. These are:
1. A non-detergent car wash liquid, specially formulated for this task
2. Two buckets with minimum 5 gal. capacity
3. A washing mitt (a second is preferred if the car is really dirty)
4. A natural or man-made chamois (you may need more than one)
5. A spray bottle of water for spot rinsing
6. Bug & Tar Remover (Turtle Wax has a good one)
7. Hose & spray nozzle
8. An assortment of short, soft bristle brushes for exterior vinyl, trim work and spoke wheels
9. Wheel cleaner specific to your wheels. (See Chapter 6 for details.)

As mentioned in the previous chapter, dishwashing soaps are formulated to remove food fats and grease, and will strip wax from your paint. Do not use them. There are several products on the shelf that are designed as washing aids containing no soap or detergent. Meguiar's,

Car wash liquids are specially formulated not to strip the wax on your paint. They also have a sudsing action designed to lift dirt off the surface so it can be wiped away easier without scratching it. Used to be dish soap was just fine, but not any longer. Make sure you dilute it properly according to the directions on the back.

Work in the shade or at the cooler times of day, like early morning or late evening. After a thorough pre-rinse, suds up the mitt as much as possible. You want a lot of sudsing action. Work in small sections, working from the top down.

Mother's and Eagle One have excellent products.

WASH TECHNIQUE

Do not wash your car in the sun if possible, and early morning or late afternoon is best if you have a choice. Most likely you have hard water with a high mineral content (unless it is filtered or softened). With this type of water, it is important that it does not dry on the paint, where it will leave a hard water mineral deposit.

Pre-Rinse

You may only need to pre-rinse the car if it is really dirty. If there is only a light film of road grime, then the extra step of pre-rinsing may not be necessary.

Pre-rinsing the car serves two purposes: it gets heavy dirt deposits off, and cools the paint. Use a strong spray for this. Be sure to work around under the body edges and dislodge as much as possible. You don't want to drag this dirt around with the wash mitt, scratching the paint as you go.

Wash Solution

To make a washing solution, place the correct amount of car wash liquid into one of the buckets as specified on the back of the product. Make sure that you dilute the solution sufficiently. If there is too much solution, it might leave a haze or film on the paint when you dry it. Measure carefully, eyeballing or "guesstimating" won't do it. Direct a strong stream of water into the container, creating an abundance of suds. Suds hold the dirt in suspension, lessening the possibility of scratching the paint as you wash it.

Procedure

Work one section of the car at a time, starting with the roof, then trunk and hood, saving vertical surfaces for last. Dip your mitt into the wash bucket, saturating it fully with a lot of suds. Wash one half of the top (one quarter if it's really dirty), applying even, medium pressure. Now, rinse the mitt in the clean water, wringing it out away from the bucket—not into the bucket. Dip your mitt in the

Using the "double dip" method of dunking in water first, then suds, to get more soap. Check the mitt periodically to make sure debris is not lodged in the folds, which could scratch the paint.

rinse with the clear water, and avoid using a hose. If you're like most people, you'll use a hose. However, flood the surface gently, making no water beads on the surface. Do not use the spray nozzle. Flooding the surfaces allows the water to "sheet" off, leaving few water rings and less water to dry. Rinse from the top down.

Wheel Wells, Wheels & Tires

Chapter 6 covers deep cleaning and detailing of your wheels and tires, so at this stage, you are just trying to remove as much surface grime and dirt as possible before going on to more caustic, specially formulated cleaners designed to remove the specific problems that attack your wheels and tires. You'll want to get any overspray from the wheels and tires over with now, before you clean, polish and wax the paint. The deep cleaning process is waterless, so you don't have to worry about messing up

washing solution again and wash the other side of the roof—then repeat rinsing the mitt. Empty and refill the rinsing bucket several times throughout the washing operation to remove all grit, which can put microscratches in the paint. Don't scrub! Remember: you don't want to scratch the surface. There's dirt on the paint and heavy scrubbing will make that dirt act like sandpaper. Keep it easy going.

Keep the bug and tar remover, as well as a separate applicator, nearby. As you wash, try rubbing the bug or tar spot off the car with the mitt. If it doesn't work, use the remover. Whatever you do, don't use the mitt with the bug & tar remover. Use a separate sponge or towel. Do not use a spare shop rag that you may have used to clean engine parts with, either. This will undoubtedly contain metal particles or other abrasives that will

scratch the paint.

Rinse—Some people use one mitt for washing, then one mitt to hand

If you run into something that's a little tough to get off, this polypropylene covered sponge can be very aggressive without scratching the paint.

Tires should be scrubbed at this stage, using a tire cleaner and wheel cleaner formulated for the task. This step is also covered in Chapter 6 as well. You can spray rinse this area.

Make sure you get up under the wheelwells.

body. A good scrub brush also works well for this. Use lots of detergent as you work on the wheels and tires. This will keep dirt in suspension and lubricate your washing mitt. This combination prevents scratching your wheels, especially painted wheels. Don't let this solution dry on the wheels (or tires).

Make sure you reach up behind the wheel and tire and get the wheel wells. This is the time to clean them, so use a scrub brush and get what you can.

Finally, rinse, rinse, rinse. You can't overrinse and you must get as much of the loose dirt and grime off as possible. Remember, we're only getting the "lumps" now—Chapter 6 covers procedures for removing things like brake fluid and dust.

your detailed paint at that stage. I suggest you use a separate washing mitt to do the tires and wheels rather than the one you'll use for the body of the car. It would be too easy to bring up some heavily soiled matter (dirt, sand, grease, or road tar) and spread it over the body or scratch the paint. So, keep a special mitt to wash the tires and wheels and one for washing the

As for final rinsing the rest of the car, don't use a high pressure spray. Flood the car's surface gently, from the top down, allowing the water to "sheet" off. This will make drying a bit faster and more uniform.

Chamois types were discussed in Chapter 1. The correct way to use the chamois is to open it up and lay it flat out on the body. Then, holding it by two of its corners, pull it across the surface. If there is a speck of dirt under it, it's less likely to scratch. Of course, there will be areas where you'll have to use it wadded up. Just remember not to scrub hard with it.

Toweling

If you don't have a chamois, then you'll have to use a towel. Or, some people like to run over the car with the chamois, then once again with a clean towel. Your choice. The professional detailers use 100% cotton terrycloth towels. Not just cotton towels, but terrycloth towels. Your bath towels are made of terrycloth to absorb water. Have you ever tried to dry off with a bed sheet? It doesn't work very well. Pros also keep all of their toweling separate. The drying towels are never mixed with the polishing towels.

Caution—In the past, steel wool scouring pads or steel wool were recommended for scrubbing wheels. But many wheels today now come with clear coat finishes that require special care. Do not use abrasives or scouring pads on these wheels.

Grilles & Exterior Trim

Grille work can be rather complex and detailed. If you have a car from the fifties you know what I mean. The easiest way to get into those cracks and crevices is with a cut-off paint brush (nylon bristles). I use a 2 1/2-inch wide paint brush with soft bristles. I use two of them: one for washing, as in the grille area and wheels; the other I use dry to brush away buffing compound and polish from around trim areas where the buffer/polisher can't reach.

Drying

You might think the next step is to wash the wheels and tires, but that is not true. Wheels and tires should be washed with special cleaners separately, as discussed in Chapter 6. The same goes for window glass. The next thing is to get the paint dry with a chamois and towels to prevent the water from drying and spotting.

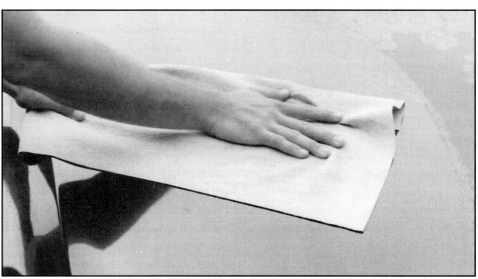

Lay the chamois out and drag it gently across the surface to get the majority of the water off.

3

PAINT INSPECTION & EVALUATION

Acid rain is perhaps one of the most common types of paint defects. If allowed to lie on your paint, it will eventually etch through the clear coat. Courtesy Meguiar's, Inc.

There are a number of environmental hazards that attack your paint on a daily basis. Some of these are man-made, others are from nature. Before you can determine the level of care your paint needs, you must first evaluate its condition and identify the various defects. First, a rundown on the contaminants that can attack your paint.

PAINT ASSASSINS

Water Spots

The very air we breathe is perhaps the worst enemy of your car's paint. As a serious amateur or professional detailer, you need to have a more qualified understanding of what chemical spots are and how they occur. By definition, chemical spotting is the discoloration or disfigurement of a painted surface due to the action of chemical

contaminants that have fallen on the surface of the paint from airborne mists and/or dusts.

In general, these contaminants are either acidic or alkaline in nature. For example, what we call acid rain is a solution of a gas such as sulfur dioxide in water that acts just like sulfuric acid on the painted surface. Or, cement dust when mixed with water is alkaline, forming a material which acts like caustic potash on the paint finish

Acid Rain—Acid rain is created when sulfur dioxide or nitrogen oxides combine with smog and water to form sulfuric and nitric acids. The etched areas on the paint can often be seen as a white ring around dulled paint. The size of the spots can vary from very small to larger than a nickel. Acid rain spots are generally rounder and more uniform than alkaline rain spots.

Alkaline Spots—Alkaline spotting

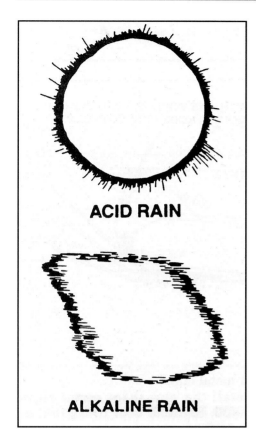

ACID RAIN

ALKALINE RAIN

Acid rain and alkaline spotting are two of the most common defects you'll find on your paint. Both must be removed to prevent etching.

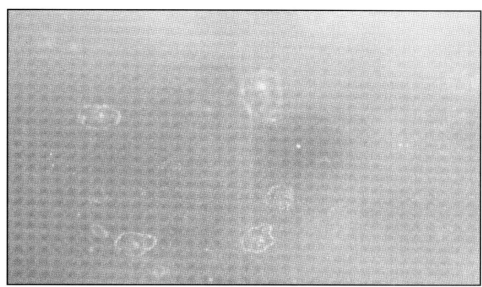

Acid rain etching. The damage is light enough to where it can be finessed out. Courtesy Meguiar's, Inc.

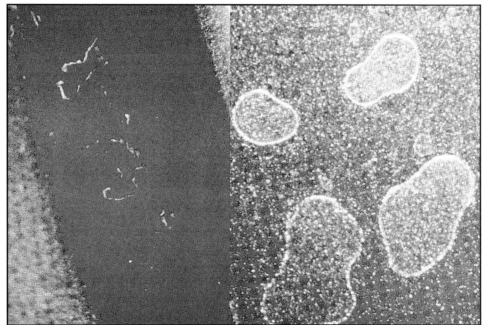

This alkaline damage is pretty severe, and probably can't be finessed out. Courtesy Meguiar's, Inc.

occurs when minerals or chemicals in water are left behind on the finish as the water dries. The gloss can be dulled in the spots and appear with a white film resembling salt deposits. If the deposits aren't cleaned off, the condition can deteriorate with later stages showing rough or jagged edges. A common cause of alkaline spotting is harsh water from sprinkler systems.

Damage Effects—When such described contaminants settle on the paint finish, two things can occur:

First, the pigment of the paint is attacked by the contaminant causing all or some area of the colors in the paint to be changed. For example, a red color (made from yellow and maroon) will increase in maroon color leaving purple, or deep red spots (if the contaminant attacks the yellow part of the red pigment).

Second, some contaminants will mark or disfigure the resin part of the paint, which results in milky or dull spotting in the form of lighter or white spots or dull patchy low gloss spots.

Susceptibility—Without exception, all paint finishes can be affected by airborne contaminants; however, some are more resistant than others. In general, the most resistant paints used today are the polyurethane clear coats whose resin system is more resistant to these contaminants. Air-dried paint finishes are more susceptible to attack than baked finishes, especially when

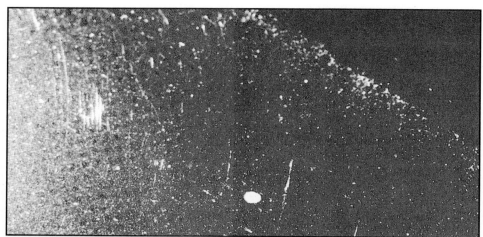

Iron particles from the rails and other source embed themselves into the paint. The spots appear like small cinders of metal sometimes surrounded by an orange stain on white paint surfaces. Courtesy Meguiar's, Inc.

the paint finish is not cured. But once cured, they are equally as resistant. The older an air-dried finish, the more resistant it becomes to chemical attack. However, neither air dry nor baked finishes are totally impervious to contaminants and the longer the contaminant remains on the surface, the greater the chance for marking, discoloration, and spotting.

In general, metallic paint jobs without clearcoat are the most susceptible to attack from airborne contaminants. This is due to the aluminum flake used, which is a reactive material when exposed to acids or alkali. But if it is clearcoated, as over 95% of metallic cars are these days, then this forms a protective barrier.

Some solid colors are also very sensitive to contaminants, and depending on the type, concentration, and the length of time it remains on the surface, these solid non-metallic colors can spot or damage also.

Chemical fallout will come from industrial sources such as effluent from the smoke stacks of manufacturing and processing facilities and oil or coal fired power

plants. The source of the contaminant can be very close to the paint finish or very far away because contaminants are wind borne, and can be released into the atmosphere where they are dissolved by moisture and returned in the form of rain on the paint surface.

The most logical protection against chemical spotting is to keep the car finish clean. This means regular washing of the car. This is important because it is difficult to notice contaminants on the paint finish. It is therefore recommended to wash the car weekly.

Thorough routine waxing of the paint finish will go a long way to help reduce chemical spotting, but it will not guarantee freedom from chemical attack. It depends largely on the type of chemical, its concentration, and the length of time it is on the finish.

Iron Particles

Most cars spend the first few days of their lives on the flatbed of a train. As the train runs over the tracks, millions of iron particles are filed off into the atmosphere, working their way into the painted surface of your car. If left alone, these tiny iron particles will rust and begin to corrode your car's sheet metal. Iron particles can be detected by feeling along the surface of the paint. The particles look black on white or light paint, gray on dark colored paint.

Cement Spots

Cement spots are dull, light gray spots on the finish which resemble mud. The lime in cement can have a high enough pH to act like paint stripper if left on the surface.

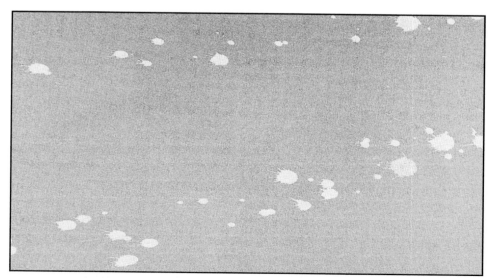

Cement can contain lime, which has a high pH. This can be as corrosive as paint stripper if not removed quickly. Courtesy Meguiar's, Inc.

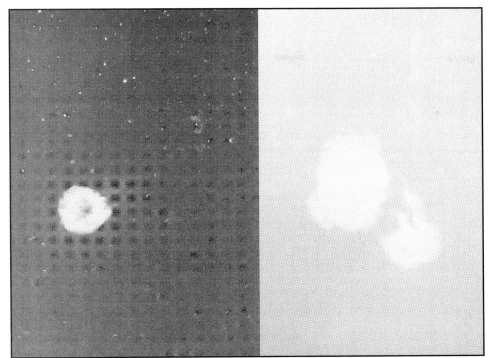

Bee pollen can quickly go from mild damage (left) to more severe damage (right). Courtesy Meguiar's, Inc.

shaped (more pointed at one end). When the bug dies, its body falls on the paint of parked cars. The body fluids in the tail are acidic and can burn into the paint if not cleaned off.

Birds

Bird droppings are a chemical brew that will eat into your car's paint within minutes. The spots are of different sizes and shapes, and etching becomes more severe the longer they stay on the finish. Can be either acidic or alkaline depending on what the bird ate.

Bat Droppings

Bat droppings take the shape of small brown spots which sometimes appear in a line. Can be even more damaging to paint than bird droppings.

Oxidation

Oxidation occurs when the exterior skin of your topcoat of paint begins to dry out. The paint finish becomes more porous, less resistant to penetration and dull. If it is not a clearcoat finish, the top coat of paint is pigmented paint that will also lighten in color as it oxidizes

Jet Fuel, Diesel Fuel, Ship Fuel

Small spots, originally oily or sooty in appearance, may be from fuel. The source could be jet, diesel or ship fuel.

Bee Pollen

These round brown or yellow spots are about 1/8" in diameter. Bee pollen and other insect droppings can actually peel the underlying paint if you try and scrape them off. Use a cleaner instead, or finesse with sandpaper.

Mayfly (Fish Fly)

Mayfly spots are crescent or "L" shaped, and can be slightly cone

Ash Spots

Ash spots come from chimneys of

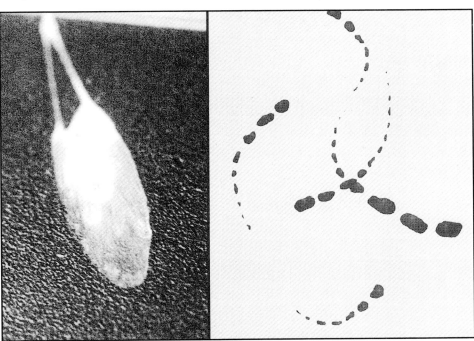

Bird droppings are shown at left, while a bat dropping is on the right. Both contain paint-eating chemicals that will cut right through the clearcoat quickly if left to stew on the paint. Courtesy Meguiar's, Inc.

These are chemical spots created by bugs that have been splattered on the hood and left to bake into the paint. Finessing with fine sandpaper, abrasive cleaners and polish are necessary to remove them. Photo by John Pfanstiehl

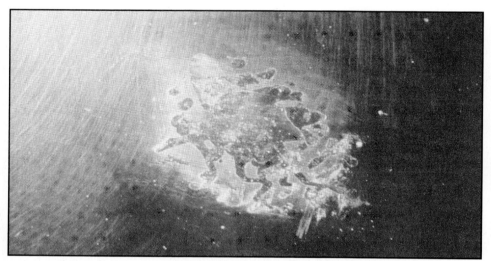

This tree sap damage has already worn through the first layer of paint, and can not be buffed out. The finish will have to be spot repainted. Courtesy Meguiar's, Inc.

The patterns of reflected light on this car clearly show what is meant by the term "swirl marks." Swirl marks are actually very fine scratches which usually result from a power buffer, hence their circular or curved pattern. The last compound or cleaner used on the paint was just a little too abrasive. The swirl marks can be removed by using a cleaner with finer abrasives, or they can be temporarily filled and hidden by some types of waxes or polishes. Photo by John Pfanstiehl

paper mills or other manufacturing plants. They are generally gray of varying size, and can be very acidic and burn deeply into paint.

Tree Sap

During spring and summer, trees release sap mist. Unlike droplets of sap, tree sap mist can travel for blocks before landing on cars passing by or parked at some distance. It's impossible to avoid, yet easy to remove when it first lands. Don't wait too long, or it will rapidly wear through the clearcoat, as shown at left.

OTHER PAINT DEFECTS

Chips, Nicks & Scratches

Other hazards are stones, opened doors, parking lot dings, and scratches. Depending on paint thickness, these can be repaired with finessing, chip repair kits, or buffed and polished out.

Swirl Marks

Swirl marks are actually very minute scratches that are caused by the power buffer cutting pad. The scratches refract light in such a way as to create the "swirl" effect. Swirl marks are often easily removed with a fine cut cleaner or mild polish.

Sunlight

Ultraviolet light is the invisible range of sunlight. The next time you view a rainbow, note that violet is the outside band. Beyond the color of violet we can see no other colors—hence, "ultra," or above, violet. For this discussion, it would serve no purpose to explore the physics of color and temperature. You simply have to have been sunburned on a

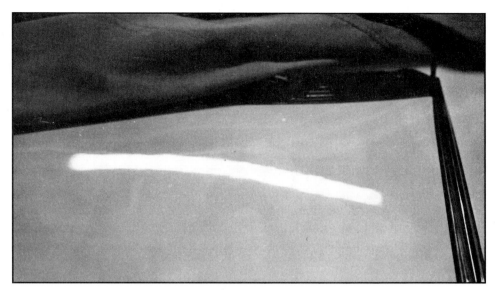

The reflection of the fluorescent light bulb in this car's finish shows a very slight wavy pattern. This can be caused by finger pressure when a sanding block isn't used. Photo by John Pfanstiehl

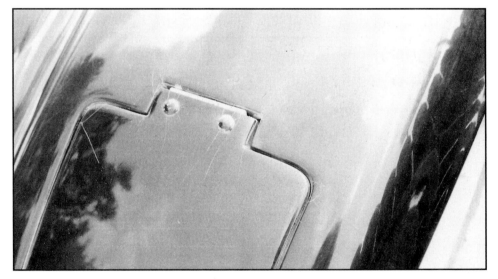

Stress cracks around hinges, as shown above, can not be finessed out. Either the paint has become brittle, or the panels are poorly supported. Photo by John Pfanstiehl

cloudy day to understand all you need to know about ultra-violet rays. What burns you also burns paint, vinyl, rubber, plastic and every other natural and man-made substance.

PAINT INSPECTION

By inspection you can evaluate the surface of your paint and determine what minimum amount of aggression will be necessary. There are three ways to evaluate the surface:

- with your hands.
- with your eyes.
- with a magnifying glass.

By Touch

At first this may seem a bit of overkill, but with a little explanation it becomes sensible. The first step will be to wash the car to remove any loose contaminants. This done, you will then run your hand over the surface of the car. What do you feel? Is the surface smooth and free of bumps—or does it feel like desert sand? Can you feel grit or do you feel oxidation. Grit would be removed one way, oxidation another. Can you feel overspray, bug droppings, road tar? Keep in mind that a well maintained paint finish is as smooth as glass. You can not have high gloss and clear reflection if your paint finish is not as smooth as glass.

Visual

Now, take a close look at the car in two kinds of light—sunlight and fluorescent light. Each of these two sources will reveal different problems. Sunlight gives hard shadows. Viewing the surface from an angle will reveal pitting (below the surface), or deposits (above the surface). Swirl marks and abrasions really show up under fluorescent or incandescent light. What do you see? Make a note and follow-up with a magnifying glass.

Photo Loupe—I use what is called a "photo loupe" for a magnifying glass. This is an especially powerful magnifying glass used by photographers to examine 35mm proofs and negatives. They come in every price range from eight dollars to $135. You set the loupe on the surface and it's automatically in focus. It's remarkable what you can see. You'll be able to see if that chip goes through the clearcoat or if that bump is road tar or a bug dropping. As you discover problems, mark the defect with a grease pencil until you decide how to take care of it.

The procedures for removing defects, restoring gloss and protecting

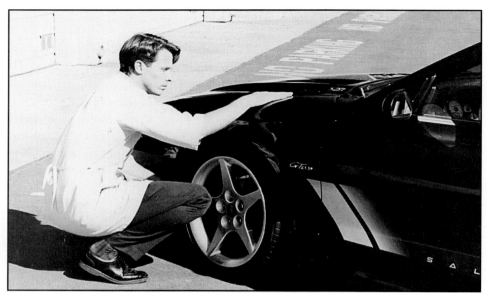

Michael Pennington of Meguiar's assesses the surface of this Saleen Mustang by running his hand over the surface to feel for contaminates. Although this is a brand new car, it sat on the dealer's lot for two days before it was brought to Meguiar's. Even in such a short period of time, plenty of contaminates, including some seagull droppings, have settled on the surface.

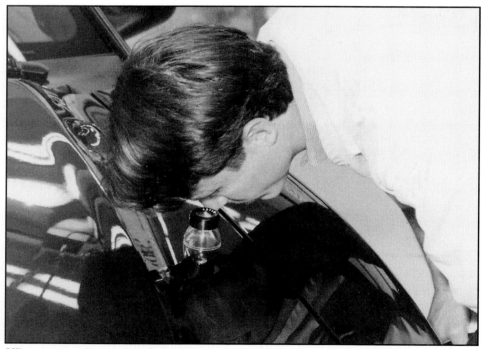

Mike next examines some of the things he found with his hand using the photographer's loupe.

paint are covered in the next chapter.

Paint Thickness

The first step is to determine whether or not the defect can be cleaned or "finessed" out, and this is mainly decided by how deep the defect is. This is determined by measuring the overall paint thickness on the car, which is measured in mils. One mil equals one thousandth of an inch, or .001". In most cases, you won't be able to finesse defects if they are more than .001" deep. It is risky to try to finesse out a defect larger than one half of a mil (.5 mil.) deep. The reason is not because it is too difficult to remove that much paint. In fact, the opposite is true.

Non-Clearcoat Finishes—In the case of a paint job that is not clear coated, the risk is that you will remove so much paint that the underlying primer will begin to show through. If the color coat is simply made too thin in spots, the color will look blotchy or show different hues in those areas. In either case, by the time you see the primer, it's too late. The damage is done to the paint and is irreversible, so repainting is the only solution.

Clearcoat Finishes—Auto manufacturers claim that new clear coat paint finishes will provide significant protection against chemical spotting by protecting the pigment. This may be true, but clear coats also present other problems. The clear coat itself is also subject to attack by chemical contaminants, which tend to leave dull or milky spots on the finish as well as pitting and etching. Of all the clear coat finishes, polyurethane enamels tend to be the most impervious to attack.

But the risk is that the clear coat will be so thin after finessing or heavy abrasive cleaning that it will provide insufficient protection of the lower layer (the color coat). The clearcoat contains sunscreens to filter out ultraviolet rays. The more of the clear surface paint is sanded or buffed off, the more UV light gets through to penetrate the underlying paint.

Checking for Clearcoat—To determine whether or not you have clearcoat (if you don't already know) rub some mildly abrasive cleaner on a rocker panel or some other

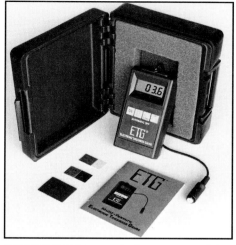
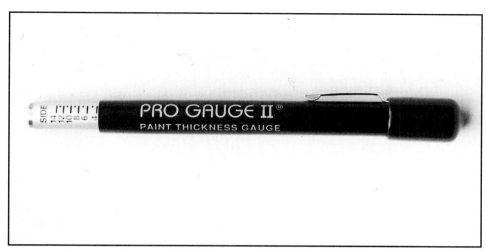

Depending on how much of a career you intend to make of this, electronic detailing gauges (above) are exceptionally accurate, and as a pro you really can't afford not to have one. But if you are only a serious enthusiast, the less expensive manual, pen-type gauges will work just as well. Both are available from Pro Motorcar Products, 813/726-9225.

inconspicuous exterior area. If your towel has color on it, then the paint is not clearcoated.

Measuring Paint Thickness

It is critical that you measure the thickness of your paint to make sure there is sufficient clearcoat and base coat, before you begin any sanding and buffing. Paint surfaces can be measured with a paint measuring gauge, such as the one offered by Pro Motorcar Products (813/726-9225). The top panels, the horizontal surfaces such as the hood, roof and trunk lid, experience much more damage from UV rays than do the sides of the cars. It only makes sense that thickness is more critical on the hood and roof than on the doors.

When measuring paint thickness, be concerned about your new car warranties or paint guarantees. In those cases, you have to go by what the car or paint manufacturer specifies if you want to preserve your warranty. You'll find some differences between the specifications of different manufacturers too. Ask the service manager or body shop manager at

your car dealer for information about what the manufacturer specifies. In the case of repainting, ask the painter or paint supply store for information on what the paint manufacturer specifies.

Thickness Guidelines—If you can't get the OEM thickness, the following general guidelines will help. In general, if the total paint thickness is between 4-5 mils (undercoat, base

coat and clearcoat combined), it is likely that an experienced or careful detailer can finesse out defects or use compound without the paint becoming too thin. To get an accurate reading, place your paint thickness gauge on the surface of the car. This is reflected off the metal of the car body and gives the thickness of the paint in mils (.001-inch). Measurements are taken randomly over the body and

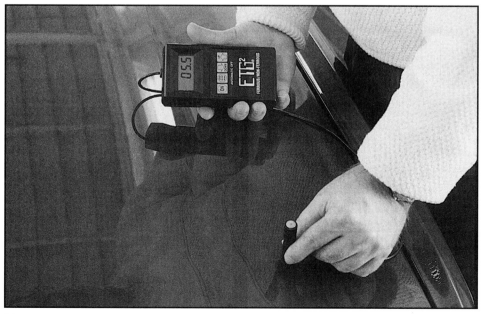

Measure around the defect in several places to make sure there is plenty of paint around the area.

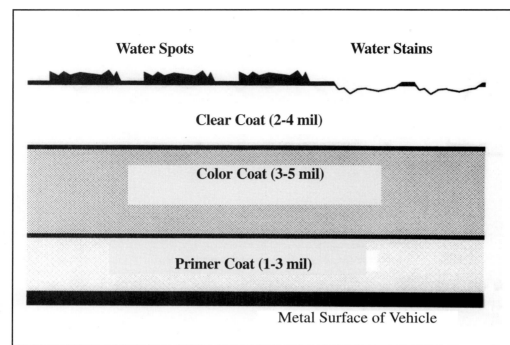

Water Spots   Water Stains

CONTAMINANT PARTICLES
Mineral Deposits

Clear Coat (2-4 mil)

Color Coat (3-5 mil)

EXPECTED DAMAGE FROM WATER SPOTS & STAINS
Primarily Surface Contamination
Possible Clearcoat Damage

Primer Coat (1-3 mil)

DEGREES OF DAMAGE
Minor = Slight Surface Contamination
Medium = Heavy Surface Contamination
Severe = Clearcoat Damage

Metal Surface of Vehicle

Cross-section paint panel with water spots and stains

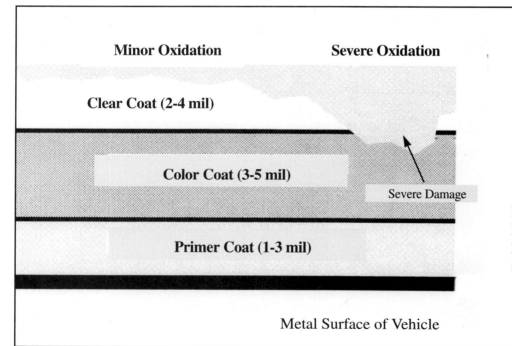

Minor Oxidation   Severe Oxidation

EXPECTED DAMAGE FROM OXIDATION
Possible Surface Contamination
Minor to Severe Clearcoat Damage
Possible Colorcoat Damage

Clear Coat (2-4 mil)

Color Coat (3-5 mil)

Severe Damage

DEGREES OF DAMAGE
Minor = Slight Clearcoat Damage
Medium = Heavy Clearcoat Damage
Severe = Colorcoat Damage

Primer Coat (1-3 mil)

Metal Surface of Vehicle

Cross section paint panel with oxidation

averaged out for a good idea of how thick the paint is.

Usually, the clearcoat is about 1.5 to 2 mils thick. (A piece of notebook paper is 2.5 mils thick.) If the average thickness of the paint job is 4.3 mils thick, you can take off as much as .5 mil and still be safe. As long as a continued average reading of the thickness gauge remained above 3.8 mils there is still 1 mil of clearcoat left. Use the following guidelines to also help gauge the thickness of your paint.

2 to 3-1/2 Mils—At two mils, the primer is about to show through on most cars, and if it is a clearcoated car, the clearcoat is nearly gone. Even

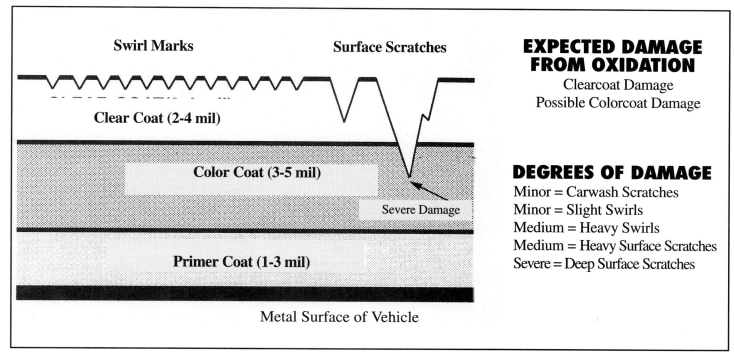

Swirl Marks Surface Scratches

Clear Coat (2-4 mil)

Color Coat (3-5 mil)

Severe Damage

Primer Coat (1-3 mil)

Metal Surface of Vehicle

EXPECTED DAMAGE FROM OXIDATION
Clearcoat Damage
Possible Colorcoat Damage

DEGREES OF DAMAGE
Minor = Carwash Scratches
Minor = Slight Swirls
Medium = Heavy Swirls
Medium = Heavy Surface Scratches
Severe = Deep Surface Scratches

Cross section of a paint panel with surface scratches or swirls

at 3 mils the paint is pretty thin, and you would be well advised to be very careful with any polishing, and forget cleaning or color sanding completely. If the paint looks good, it may have years of life left if it can avoid prolonged exposure to the sun and elements.

3-1/2 to 5-1/2 Mils—This is the normal range of most factory paint jobs. One of the most conclusive tests is to look for variation in the paint thickness around the car. Although it's possible to find as much as 1 1/2 mil variation on one panel (such as a door), if all of the car reads close to 4 mils and one fender reads 6, that is evidence that the fender was repainted.

5-1/2 to 7-1/2 Mils—It still may be factory paint but on many cars paint which measures this thick indicates repainting has occurred. If it is a two-tone car, one color may have been painted over the other at the factory and the thickness may exceed 6 mils

on that overlaying color. Look closely for overspray on moldings or tape lines on door jams.

7-1/2 to 9-1/2 Mils—It is almost certainly repainted but the finish may last if the vehicle is garaged, is a northern car, or if it has urethane top coats over a good base. Few paint manufacturers would recommend painting over paint this thick.

Damage Levels

Damage can be categorized into several levels.

Level 1—This level would indicate no damage beyond surface contamination left from iron particles or other industrial fallout, and swirl marks.

Level 2—Minor damage, the contamination did not penetrate more than 0.5 mil of the top coat or clearcoat. Abrasive cleaning with a heavy compound, followed by polishing, is recommended, as is some sanding. Light scratches, heavy

chemical etching are types of level two damage.

Level 3—This is substantial damage, where the contamination has penetrated to a depth of more that .5 mils of the top or color coat. Recolor/clearcoat is necessary to fix this.

GLOSS METER

In spite of all the new buffers, bonnets, tools, papers, and procedures, one vital step was still missing from the process of evaluating and improving paint finishes. Until now, the only means of rating the quality of a finish at a body shop, dealership, or car lot has been subjective. Whether a finish was acceptable or whether it matched the other panels has always been an opinion, and everyone has a different opinion.

For the first time since paper and polish have been taken to a car's finish, there is an affordable means for shops to measure the quality of the paint's surface finish. This breakthrough was unveiled at I-CAR's International Meeting in Pittsburgh this August and ABRN is the first publication to disclose it to the refinish industry.

The instrument measures "Distinctness of Image Gloss," which is a higher level of perception than a single parameter such as gloss. A brief explanation is that the visual perception of an auto finish involves many things other than gloss. Gloss is defined as the amount of light reflected off a surface. If an orange was chrome-plated, it would have excellent gloss, but a person wouldn't rate its finish as being excellent. That's one of the reasons why gloss meters have been unable to successfully discriminate the quality of Class A automotive finishes.

The new Quality of Finish Measurement (QFM) instrument (shown below) is a small hand-held battery powered instrument which enables measurement and evaluation of automotive finishes. It can be used in the shop or outside at car lots. Driver's Mart Worldwide is already using this to establish the first objective finish standards for both the purchasing and the reconditioning of its cars.

This new technology is the missing link which will enable shops to objectively measure the effect on top coat finishes made by changing processes or products in application of paint or in sanding and buffing. It can also be used to more closely match the finish quality of refinished panels to the adjacent OEM finished panels. And finally it permits an individual shop to set measurable finish standards which can be demonstrated to be above the OEM level, or above the competition. The QFM is available from Pro Motorcar Products at 813/726-9225.

4

PAINT CLEANING, POLISHING & WAXING

This is the type of finish you should be striving for. A professional detail job, one that entails cleaning, polishing and waxing the paint, brings out a deep glossy "wet" look that turns heads on the street and at the car show. **Photo by Michael Lutfy**

The next step, after identifying the surface defect, is to get rid of it. Your approach is going to be based on how deep the defect is, and how thick the paint is around it.

Throughout this book, I stress the "less is best" approach favored by many detailing professionals. This means trying the least aggressive, or least abrasive method to remove a defect before going to the next step. The less paint or clearcoat you have to remove, the better. There is a finite amount of material (paint, clearcoat, vinyl, plastic, chrome and other finishes) on your car. No matter how gentle you are with these finishes, some of it comes off each time you deep clean or compound the paint. Work long enough and all of it will come off. Therefore, the more aggressive the compound you use, the faster the finish will disappear. To reduce this problem, use the least abrasive material possible,

commensurate with the condition of the problem you're working on. According to Mike Pennington of Meguiar's, harsh rubbing compounds from years ago represent technology that is outdated for today's high tech paint finishes, and they should be avoided. There are newer formulations that redefine what has traditionally been known as compounding, and they are just as effective. However, a good rule of thumb is that if you can avoid having to use a heavy cutting or cleaning compound, by all means, move ahead to page 43 and go right to polishing and waxing. If not, then read on.

REMOVING MINOR DEFECTS

Before you get out the buffer and a gritty abrasive to remove a bird dropping, splattered bug or road tar, try to remove the defect with some plain old bug and tar remover, or 3M's

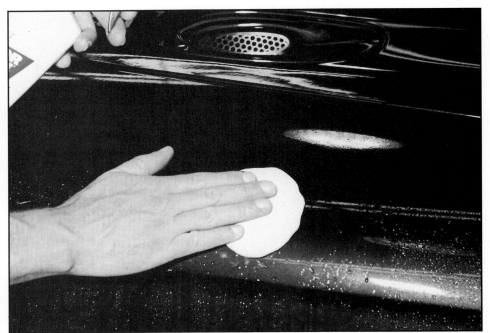

Detailing or fallout clay should be used first before going on to buffing with an abrasive cleaner. It is particularly effective for removing light surface defects caused by industrial fallout. Apply a lubricant such as car wash soap directly to the spot, make a "hamburger patty" of the clay, and rub lightly over the surface.

When it comes to buffing, you just can't get the same results you would by hand. Orbital polishers, on the other hand, are really just labor-saving devices. From left to right is shown a double-action buffer (relatively safe for use by the novice), an orbital buffer (completely safe) and a rotary buffer (very easy to burn paint with, even for a professional). But for deep cleaning of defects, you're going to need a rotary buffer.

Detailing Clay

You can now decontaminate the exterior surfaces of the vehicle by removing all industrial fallout, overspray and rail dust that naturally accumulate over time, with detailing or fallout clay. The clay is used with a lubricant, or with car wash soap to safely and inexpensively remove light surface contamination. The previous method of choice was to use an acid solution to wash the surface of the vehicle and remove approximately 80% of the contaminants. This method was used for many years and proved to be rather dangerous. The risk of staining parts of the vehicle was very high. Detailing clay is virtually risk free and produces much higher quality results by removing almost all contaminants. With our "less is best approach," you may be able to remove some pretty heavy defects without using heavy cleaners and go right to polishing.

Procedure—Wash the entire vehicle if you have not already done so. The paint surface should be cool to the touch prior to beginning. Use a properly labeled safety bottle to apply a light mist of the clay lubricant, or soap suds, to an area no larger than 3' by 3' with properly diluted car wash soap. Form the clay into a pancake shape for easy application. Rub it over the surface of the vehicle with light pressure. Increase pressure as needed to remove all surface contaminants. Wipe the section with a soft towel to remove the lubricant, then feel the surface with your hand. If the surface is smooth and free of below surface defects, such as oxidation or light scratches, then you can move to the polishing step, page 43. If you still feel there are particles then repeat the

General Purpose Adhesive Remover. Remember the "less is best" approach. This should be attempted during the washing process, because these solutions should not be allowed to dry on the paint. If you've already washed, just make sure to rinse the spot with clean water to remove any residual remover. Apply the remover to a terrycloth towel, and attempt to remove it. If it doesn't come off after three tries (no more) then go on to the next step, which would be to attempt removing it with a mild abrasive.

If you are purchasing a buffer and have a shop compressor, consider an air-powered model. The biggest advantage is that they are significantly lighter than their electrical cousins. If you are going to spend long hours buffing, this may be worth serious consideration. Photo by John Pfanstiehl.

damage is to the paint. Meguiar's, Eagle One, P&S and others have their own system of abrasiveness, both for products and pads.

Rotary Buffer—It is impossible to achieve the same level of results by hand that are possible with a rotary buffer. This is particularly true for cleaning. It is only logical that a buffing pad spinning at 1200 to 3000 rpm's combined with the weight and downward pressure of the buffer is infinitely more effective for cleaning than anything you can do by hand. The downside, of course, is that it is easy for a high speed rotary buffer to burn paint in the hands of an inexperienced operator. When used improperly it can cut through clear coat, base coat, sanding sealer, primer, and right into the metal—before you can even release the trigger! It's my suggestion that you learn to use this piece of equipment on a scrap piece of metal before you use it on your car.

Buffing Pads—Available for this machine are a wide variety of buffing pads which include various densities of polyurethane foam and sheepskin. The foam pads are a rather new product, developed in the '80's and heavily used in the '90's. Before them,

clay process until all surface contaminants have been removed. After completing each section fold the putty in half and form a new pancake. Complete this process over the entire exterior painted surfaces of the vehicle. If there are still further defects, then we must go to the next most abrasive method.

ABRASIVE CLEANING

The least abrasive methods have not worked, so we must move on to the next step. We are now into the realm of removing part of the painted surface, whether it is with a heavy abrasive compound, or with ultrafine sandpaper to finesse out defects. Before you can accurately choose a method of treatment, you need to know how thick the paint is on your car. Refer to Chapter 3 to determine the paint thickness on your car, and the severity of the defect.

Defect Removal

Now that you've determined there is

enough paint on the car to remove heavy oxidation, light scratches or acid etching, the next step, following our "less is best" mandate, is to try an abrasive compound on a variable speed buffer. At this stage, you must choose a cleaner and pad suitable for the amount of damage to the paint. Unfortunately, the variety of systems used by all of the various manufacturers does not allow for any set hard and fast rules. Also, only you can truly determine how severe the

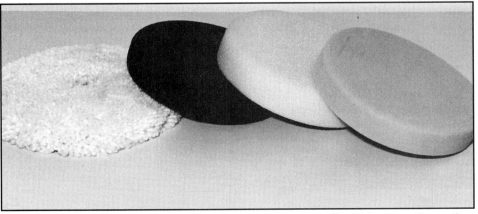

From left to right: a wool bonnet normally used with the rotary buffer for heavy cutting action. The other three are foam pads which can be used with all three machines shown in the photo on the opposite page. These pads come in three colors: burgundy, which is used for the heaviest cutting; yellow, a light cutting pad; and tan, used for polishing only.

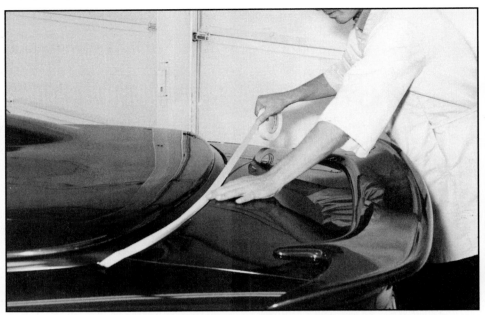

Edges around doors, trunk lids and hoods have the thinnest coats of paint. To prevent burning through these areas with a power buffer, place a strip of masking tape over every edge. When finished, you'll have to remove the tape and polish these areas by hand.

Side panels are a bit more difficult because of the angle. One helpful tip is to get down as level as possible to the area you are buffing. The tendency, because of the angle, is to apply too much pressure, so be careful that you don't.

Getting the proper buffing technique down will take some practice. The pros (like Meguiar's Director of Training, Mike Pennington, above), lay down a stripe of cleaner about 12 inches long, then start the buffer, then sweep across the stripe from right to left, with the leading edge of the pad tilted up a bit until you make contact, then lay the pad flat. Keep your touch light, and let the machine do the work for you. Don't let it stop moving, or it will burn through the paint before you know it. Note how Mike keeps the cord from wrapping up in the buffer by slinging it over his shoulder. Also, note that he is wearing eye protection, which is always a good idea.

agent works. With a good compound and the right wool pad, the worst oxidation (and sometimes paint job) can quickly be removed. With the foam bonnet and a good swirl mark remover—and a very deft touch—even the lightest swirl marks can be eliminated.

To use this machine, spread or pour a few tablespoons of product onto the surface of the car, a single stripe about 12 inches long, and begin by turning the machine on slowly, about half speed. Then sweep across the stripe right to left, with the leading edge of the pad tilted up a little bit. Then place the machine flat and continue to buff.

Hold the buffer firmly. Its great speed and heavy mass will do two things when it starts. It tends to jump and twist from centrifugal force. Using it requires a great deal of finesse.

With the machine running, it is best to keep the pad flat at all times, even

only the sheepskin pad was available. Each pad is designed to do a job with

a certain product. Most of this is based on how aggressively the cutting

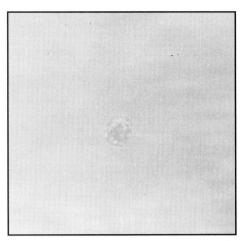

1. This acid rain spot is a common example of the type of chemical defect that can be eliminated or dimished with finessing techniques. These procedures also work well with bird droppings, alkaline spots or tree sap. Photo by John Pfanstiehl

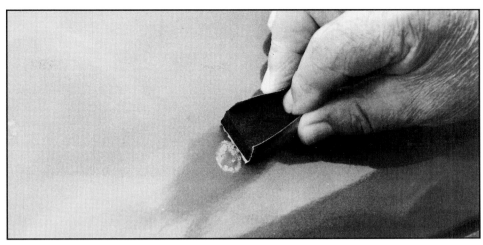

2. Try removing the spot with fallout clay, bug and tar remover or a polish first (remember less is best). If this doesn't work, try block sanding with 2000-grit paper. Use plenty of water and flush off any particles of the defect that may break off. Photo by John Pfanstiehl

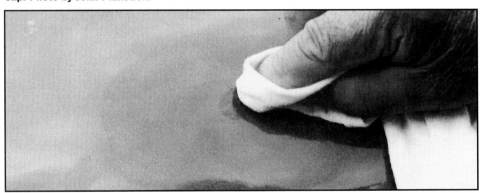

3. The sanding will quickly tell you whether the crust is only on the surface of the paint or has etched down into it deeply. In this case, the etching was deep and completely sanding it out would have risked taking off too much paint. Use a fine polish to bring back the paint's gloss. Photo by John Pfanstiehl

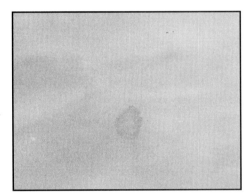

4. Although the spot is still visible, it is much more noticeable. The sanding and cleaning also removed any traces of paint damaging chemicals, to ensure that etching and damage to the paint won't continue. Photo by John Pfanstiehl

with the work area. Use overlapping strokes. This is the way the pros do it. If you fight the machine and try to force it in a direction it doesn't want to go, you'll make it do your bidding but your back and shoulders will pay! Keep your touch light. Let the machine do the work for you, and never, ever let it set in one place for even an instant. It will burn right through the paint before you can stop it!

Once more I must caution you to learn to use this machine on a paint surface that doesn't matter to you so you can learn what the limits are before the buffer will burn paint. Don't let your first lesson be on a $4000 custom paint job!

FINESSING

The above process was the next, least abrasive method to remove a defect. If there is still a defect that is etched deeper, it is possible that it may be finessed out with sandpaper. The technique used to finesse paint is similar to color sanding. The difference is, finessing refers to

removing a single defect on an isolated or small area, while the whole car is generally color sanded, and only then to remove orange peel and restore gloss. However, the sanding papers and technique are the same.

Sanding

After inspection of the defect, and after taking several paint thickness readings around the defect, the next step is sanding. "Sanding" might actually be too strong a term because the new types of sandpaper used in

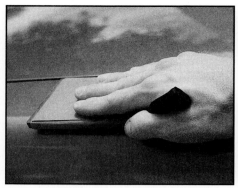

A new type of sanding block has been designed to produce the flattest finishes. The Pro Block has a spring steel core which distributes pressure evenly and thereby eliminates the finger grooves common to other flexible sanding blocks. A thumb tab gives better control when sanding, and helps keep it from slipping out of your hand when wet-sanding. Photo by John Pfanstiehl.

The PrepPen is a new type of sanding tool which has a bundle of fiberglass bristles to permit cleaning in areas where sandpaper, other brushes or solvents can't reach. It's useful for cleaning aluminum, fasteners, and cleaning paint defects such as acid rain spots to determine the depth of the damage. Photo by John Pfanstiehl.

Meguiar's has abrasive sanding blocks as fine as 2000-grit available. They are good for sanding small defects in a paint's finish. Photo by John Pfanstiehl.

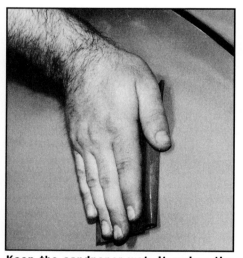

Keep the sandpaper wet. It makes the sandpaper cut better and last longer. Unlike the fellow in this photo, use a sanding block to avoid making ridges with your fingers. Photo by John Pfanstiehl

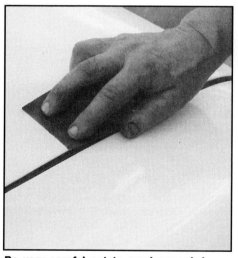

Be very careful not to sand around doors, hoods, and trunk lids. These areas have very little paint, so you will break through to primer in a hurry if you try to sand along them. Photo by Jim Richardson

finessing are really more like "polishing papers." The finest grit available used to be 600-grit, but now grits of 1000, 1500, and 2000 (often called microfine and ultrafine) are common. It is best to use the finest paper possible that will still remove the defect. Start with 2000-grit paper, especially if you are a beginner. If that doesn't remove the defect, then move up to 1500-grit and so on.

The 1500- and 2000-grit papers are so fine and they remove paint so slowly that you can actually remove paint faster with a buffer using a wool pad and polishing compound. Then why use them? Control. A few thousandths of an inch can make the difference between saving a paint job and having to pay for a new one. By using microfine sandpapers with a sanding block, you can remove paint

steadily and uniformly. However, if a power buffer is being used for polishing, professionals will sand with a coarser paper, from 1000- to 1200-grit. If you haven't had much experience, however, be very careful using 1000-grit or a buffer. Both can remove a lot of paint very quickly.

Sanding Block—Fold the paper around a thin, flexible rubber sanding block. If a sanding block is not used, the pressure of your fingers will create ruts in the paint. Even though these ruts are very shallow, they can show up in reflected light and produce a wavy, patchy appearance on the paint's finish.

It is best to use a sanding block during finessing but there are cases where it can be omitted. For example, if there is one particularly deep defect, such as a sunken or pitted spot, and you don't want to risk sanding the surrounding paint down too far, use just one finger to sand that spot.

Wet-Sanding—Wet-sanding helps the paper last longer and helps it cut through the paint better. Keep the paper and the paint wet during sanding to prevent the paper from getting clogged up with the removed paint. Thoroughly clean out a bucket to remove any sand or grit and then

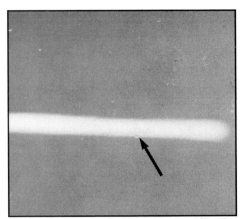

1. You'll be surprised at how easily the smallest surface irregularities will be visible under the proper lighting. The reflection of overhead fluorescent tubes is best for spotting small details. This pot-marked area, visible in the light's reflection, looks pretty bad up close but is only about two ten-thousandths of an inch in depth (.2 mils). (Photos 1-6 by John Pfanstiehl)

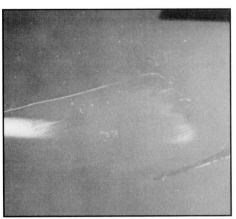

2. Clean the surface to remove any sand or dirt. Then splash on some water and lightly sand with 2000-grit paper. Squeegee the water off with a soft pliable rubber block to check your progress. Move around to find the best angle for viewing the area. Any remaining low points will be quite visible as shiny dots.

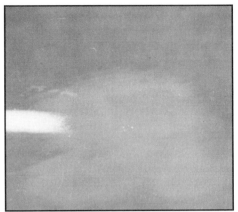

3. After less than a minute of sanding only a few low points remain. If you polish this area now, it will look much better than before but the remaining points will be visible under close examination in the proper light. It's a judgment call about how far to sand because you never know when you will break through the clearcoat, or color coat. If the rest of your car is not show car perfect it may be wise to stop while you're ahead.

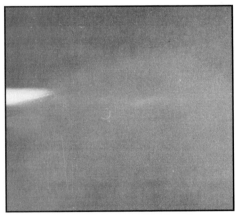

4. After the paint defect is removed to your satisfaction, wipe the area clean. Placing a piece of tape in line with the defect at the start helps make it easier to inspect that area during the process. As you sand, the area you're covering typically gets bigger and bigger, and sometimes it's hard to remember exactly where the defect was located.

5. Use a clean, soft cotton cloth and fine polishing compound to remove the tiny sanding scratches left from the 2000-grit paper. A fresh unused section of the paper removes paint relatively quickly and leaves deeper scratches. After it has been used a little while, it becomes duller. A worn piece "cuts" slower but it leaves only very minute sand scratches. If you have a well worn piece available, use it to do the final sanding. After using the polishing compound the reflection will return but it's still a little hazy from scratches left by the very fine abrasives.

6. Polish the area with a separate soft cloth using Meguiar's Heavy Duty Car Cleaner. The photo doesn't do justice to the increase in gloss and brilliance this last step accomplishes. If the sanding was done with a sufficiently worn piece of 2000-grit paper, try skipping the polishing compound and go right to the cleaner. Finish with a wax if you desire.

fill it halfway with water. Add a few drops of dish detergent to help keep the paper from gumming up.

Rinse the paper and surface frequently while sanding. I can't stress the importance of this too much because if a speck of grit or accumulated paint builds up, the scratches it will leave will be far deeper than those of the sandpaper. The problem is that such deep scratches won't be noticed until the polishing stage is done; and then the paint will have to be sanded again, resulting in the removal of more paint. To prevent these scratches, frequently check the surface of the sandpaper for any buildup or traces of grit.

It's a good idea to continually bathe the areas you are sanding with a small stream of water from a garden hose. If the hose has a metal connector on its end, cover the metal part with tape to prevent it from chipping or scratching the paint.

Sand in one direction, polish in another direction (typically at right angles). By doing this, any remaining scratches can be identified to see which step is creating the problem.

If you want to remove very small defects or pits, mark the spot with tape or other means. When you are working in the middle of a panel, it's easy to get off base an inch or two. By marking the spot, you also save time when you try to find and inspect the spot as it becomes smaller.

Use a second rubber block as a squeegee, and wipe the area every minute or so. When the water is wiped off, the remaining small pits show up as shiny spots and this makes them much more visible.

Remember that sandpapers do wear out and load up. You'll notice as it doesn't cut any more, or that you have to press harder to get the same sanding effect. This could result in deeper scratches, which is exactly what you are trying to avoid. Now's the time to use some fresh sandpaper.

Worn sandpaper can be useful, in finessing, particularly when the job is done by hand. Use fresh pieces of paper to sand out the defects; then clean the surface and go over it with a well-worn piece of sandpaper. Such paper is so fine that it acts like a fine polishing compound, and it can even leave a bit of a gloss to the paint. Worn paper removes the deeper scratches left by the fresh paper, and using it can sometimes save one step in the polishing process.

PAINT CHIP REPAIR

Although some may argue that

DETAILING A NEW PAINT JOB
by John Pfanstiehl

By new paint job, we're talking about a custom or bodyshop repaint, not the OEM paint job from the factory. There are so many options at every stage in sanding and buffing a new top coat, where does one begin? Here's one shop's procedure and I'll bet it has a step which most shops have never tried. And this step can be a real time-saver. Final Finish in Branford, Connecticut, specializes in high-end restorations (if you consider cars like supercharged Bugatti roadsters high end) and refinishes many of the custom Calloway supercars. This is a five step process which owner David SeCaur is first to point out is far more than is needed for most refinish work.

1. Wet-sand all orange peel out with 1000 grit paper after waiting 2 or 3 days. The waiting period is very important because once the topcoat fully cures sanding and buffing is MUCH more difficult. Even though the paint manufacturer says wait 24 hours, Dave has found that no matter what the air temperature, it's still too soft after only one day. He is careful to schedule the final clear coating so that time is available 2 or 3 days later for the sanding and buffing.
2. Wet-sand the 1000 grit sand scratches out with 1500 grit or 2000 grit (Norton) paper. At both sanding stages, he uses a sanding block with spring steel core. The very last sanding involves going lightly over the entire surface with 1500 or 2000 grit paper without the block.
3. Buff with a 1.5 inch thick wool pad (Schlegel 875C) and 3M 06021.
4. Buff with lambs wool pad (Schlegel 904) and 3M 05992.
5. Polish with a foam pad (3M 05725) and 3M 05996 Polish Glaze.

Most shops will be able to use combinations of other papers, pads and polishes to streamline the topcoat sanding process to a four-step or even three-step process for most of their applications. This is one area where it pays to experiment and try new products.

---

repairing paint chips is the realm of the bodyman, we beg to differ. Here's an area of car maintenance, like keeping sufficient oil in your engine or sufficient air in your tires, where a little care prevents costly future damage. Car enthusiasts will want to fix chips to keep their finish looking great but there's also a strong functional and economic reason to repair paint chips.

A chip in automotive paint frequently goes down to the bare metal of the car's body. Even if it only goes down to the primer, the primer is usually not a thick enough barrier to prevent rusting. The primer promotes adhesion of the paint to the body panels; the color coat (of base coat/clearcoat paint) is for purely cosmetic reasons, and it is up to the top coat to provide protection from the elements. When there's a break in the armor of the top coat, the

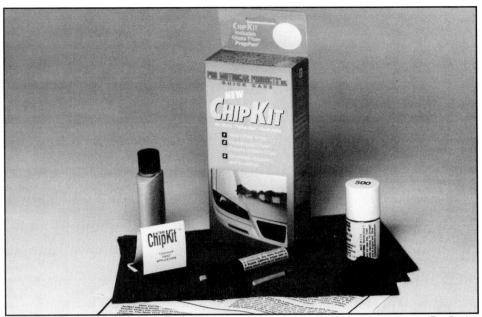

1. Paint chip repair is convenient and easy with this all-in-one kit from Pro Motorcar Products. The ChipKit™ contains the PrepPen, clearcoat paint, a sanding block, applicators, 2 sheets each of 1500- and 2000-grit sandpaper and a fine polishing compound. All you need to do is get the proper touch-up paint for your vehicle. It's available at GM dealers and direct from Pro Motorcar at 813/726-9225. By the way, the PrepPen brush also works for many detailing tasks such as cleaning aluminum parts and hard to get at areas. Photos 1-8 by John Pfanstiehl

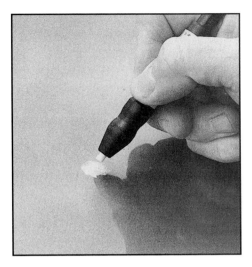

2. Begin by thoroughly brushing the chip with firm pressure. The glass fibers in the brush won't scratch or scrape the surrounding paint, but they will degloss it. This prepares the surface so the touch-up paint will stick. TIP: Wait a few days between successive applications of touch-up paint, and then lightly brush the area clean and prep it before applying the new coats of paint.

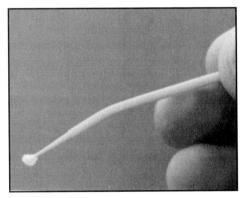

3. Shake or stir the touch-up paint for a minute, or longer in the case of metallics. ProTouch is a microsized brush which has non-absorbent fibers at the end to precisely apply small quantities of paint, or remove it if too much is applied. You can also use the trimmed end of a paper match, which works much better than the cheap brush that comes with the touch-up paint.

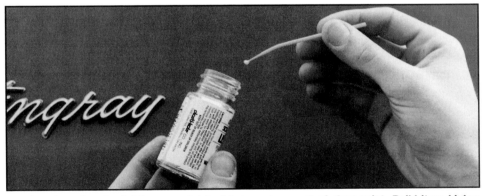

4. After the colored paint has completely dried, apply a coat of clear paint. Build it up higher than the surrounding finish, so several applications will probably be necessary. The paint will shrink down as the solvents evaporate. TIP: Store your touch-up paint or leftover paint upside down. If there's a small airleak at the cap, the paint will seal it so the remaining paint won't dry out. (Continued on next page).

underlying paint and body panels are prone to deterioration.

The corrosion and damage can progress to become much larger than the original chip. Check your car's rust-through warranty. It may stipulate that all paint chips must be repaired or the warranty is void. Even if your car doesn't have a rust-through warranty, the meaning should be clear—it is important to fix paint chips. Today's cars use thinner sheet metal than ever before to decrease weight and increase fuel economy. On modern cars, it doesn't take long for a paint chip to rust completely through a body panel.

There are a number of other reasons to repair chips in the surface paint. For example, some bumpers and fascia parts are constructed of a flexible material that can be damaged by constant exposure to UV radiation from the sun. Even if the entire part is stripped and repainted later, the exposed areas may become more brittle and deteriorate more rapidly.

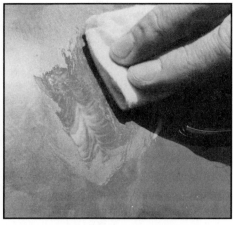

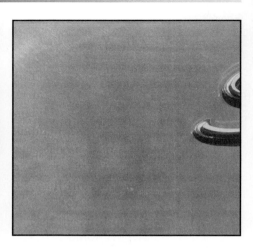

5. Allow the paint to dry for a day or more. If the touch-up paint has remained higher than the surrounding paint over the entire area of the chip, it's time to block-sand the repair. Use 1500-grit paper and switch to 2000-grit when the area becomes smooth. Use plenty of water to clean the paper and surface every few strokes. Check to make sure the paint isn't balling up on the sandpaper.

6. Use an ultra-fine polishing compound on a soft cloth to bring back the shine. If you can still see very fine scratches or swirl marks, next try using a car cleaner polish, which has even finer abrasives. Some cleaner-waxes will work well also.

7. The end result will be a smooth repair which is hard to see if the touch-up color was a close match. By making the repair flush with the surrounding finish, there are no edges to interrupt and distort the reflections on your paint.

Most paint chips can be repaired without repainting the entire panel. Repainting panels can present some problems, which will be discussed shortly, and therefore should only be done as a last resort. The original factory paint is usually very durable and therefore should be repaired and preserved when the damage is simply small chips or nicks. The illustration sequence on pages 41-43 illustrates the step-by-step procedure.

Touch-Up Paint

Whenever your car is being repainted, remember to think ahead. Make sure to get a bottle of touch-up paint from the same batch used to paint your car, if at all possible, to use for paint chip repair because matching paint is more difficult than it used to be.

But if you're like most car owners, you will not have touch-up paint on hand from a recent paint job, nor are you likely to have some from the factory. Therefore, you will have to hunt down the proper color touch-up

paint to repair paint chips and scratches. New car dealerships are a good place to look, not because the paint is any better, but because they should have the color in stock.

Buying touch-up paint at a dealership does not guarantee the paint will be a perfect match, however. As mentioned before, the touch-up paint you buy, whether it be a one-ounce bottle or a quart can, is different than the paint the factory sprayed on your car. Furthermore, it is likely the manufacturer of the touch-up paint is not the same manufacturer of the factory paint.

And, in the case of cars with base coat/clear coat paint, you wouldn't want the original paint anyway. The color coat (base coat) applied at the factory was specifically formulated to add the color and cover the underlying primers. It is not weather-resistant by itself and is often dull in finish. Most base coat paints need a clear coat for protection and to provide gloss. Many base coats today are water-borne paints which are then covered with an additional urethane clear paint. However, touch-up paint is usually a

lacquer-based paint to permit easy application and fast drying with only one step.

There are so many automotive colors today that before driving to a dealership it is wise to call the parts department to see if they have the right color on hand. It costs a lot to keep a large inventory of paint, so don't be surprised if a dealership or parts store doesn't have your color on the shelf. The counter person may know immediately which paint you need if you tell them the model and year of the car and describe the color, for example, "dark blue metallic."

Paint Codes—The paint code is a number assigned by the car manufacturer to a particular color. This is often needed to locate the proper color paint. The paint code is written on a tag located on the car's body. To find the location of the tag, look for a book attached to the display of touch-up paints. Inside will be diagrams showing where to look for the code on the various models of cars, and then there will be a table to cross-reference the car manufacturer's code with the number on the bottle so

8. Once all of the defects have been removed, move to the polishing stage. If you used a rotary buffer, chances are there are swirl marks. You'll need a product formulated to remove swirls, or a fine polish.

that you can select the closest color.

Unfortunately, you'll find that some factory paint codes today list four or more variances—different looking mixtures from which you have to choose the best match. The variation in color in some factory paint codes is one reason why buying touch-up paint from the car dealership or getting "factory packs" of premixed-mixed paint is no assurance of getting a close match. Therefore, always check the match of the paint before driving away. Shake the paint very thoroughly because the metallics and even the color pigment can settle to the bottom of the bottle after being on the shelf for several months. Apply a little touch-up paint on a clean area of the car to check for color match. If there is no area on the outside of the car where you wish to test the color match, open the trunk or hood or try the door jambs. Check the color match after it has dried.

Tools

Although the touch-up paint you buy today is not much different than touch-up paint made 10 years ago, there are new methods of preparing the chipped area before application of the paint. It is critical to get into the chipped area and clean out any wax, dirt, or road film so that the touch-up paint can adhere and seal off the chip. It is equally important to clean out any loose surface rust because it traps air and moisture and allows the rusting to continue even after it is covered up by paint.

A new tool which is remarkably effective at both cleaning out rust and wax, silicones, or road grime is the Prep Pen Brush. The tip is composed of a bundle of fiberglass bristles each smaller in diameter than a human hair. The bristles permit a strong, almost pinpoint cleaning and scrubbing of a paint chip or scratch. The fiberglass is strong enough to scrub off surface rust yet it doesn't chip or scratch the

surrounding paint. However, it does scuff the original paint to promote adhesion of the touch-up paint.

A different type of tool is 3M's Rust Avenger, which is a chemical that converts surface rust into something better to paint over. It doesn't remove rust scale or any accumulations of wax, salt, or films. And obviously it is not for use on non-metal panels such as aluminum, plastic, fiberglass, or rubber body parts.

Cleaning a small chip or scratch with sandpaper is better than no preparation at all, but be careful not to sand down the surrounding paint too far while trying to get at the edges of the chip or scratch. Also be careful if you use a pointed tool such as a screwdriver or ice pick to scrape out a chip because it is easy to slip and create a deeper scratch or scrape next to the chip. For a step-by-step demonstration on repairing paint chips, see the sidebars on the previous two pages.

POLISHING

Many cars, especially newer ones or those well maintained, begin their exterior detailing process here. They only need a minor abrasive polish and a coat of wax to restore their luster. If the vehicle is new from the factory, or has just been repainted in a body shop, there may be orange peel present, which must be color sanded out to achieve a true deep gloss.

If you have just finished deep cleaning, or finessing defects, then you'll certainly need to polish the paint as the next step. After the gloss has been restored, it will need to be protected with wax.

The terms polishing and waxing refer to two entirely separate functions

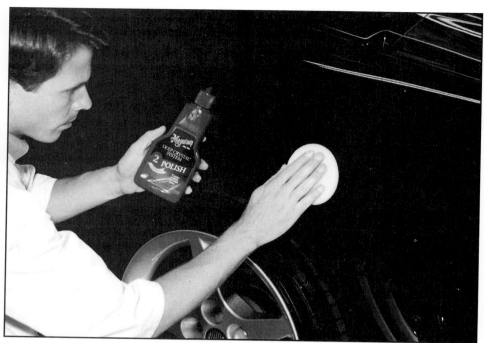

Mike Pennington of Meguiar's is applying a mild, fine polish with a foam pad to the panel of this late-model Mustang. It doesn't need a lot of gloss restoration, so he doesn't need a heavy-cut polish. An orbital polisher can be used to save labor.

at least once a month and want to avoid having a wax build-up; and, (3) those who want to improve the appearance of a freshly re-painted finish without fear of inhibiting the curing process during the first 30 days.

All paint finishes, when neglected, will degrade and oxidize over time...caused primarily by UV penetration. While today's clear coat paint finishes include UV inhibitors, the process still continues—albeit much more slowly than in past years. Without question, regular applications of a pure polish is the absolute best way to prevent oxidation. Much like a rich body lotion nourishes your skin, a pure polish nourishes the paint, keeping it healthy and vibrant. In other words, a pure polish can keep your paint finish as healthy as it was when it was first painted—before it ever had a chance to dry out and oxidize. If the paint finish on your car is already clean and smooth as glass, regular applications of a pure polish

which are not interchangeable. The classic and correct definition of polishing refers to the creation of high gloss. Polishing diamonds, as an example, is done to achieve added brilliance—without any thought of adding protection. Waxing, on the other hand, is part of the larger category of "protection" which involves the application of a barrier coat of waxes, polymers, resins and silicones on top of paint finishes to protect them from the elements.

A car that has just been painted portrays deep, clear reflections and vibrant high gloss before it is ever polished or waxed. The goal, therefore, is to keep your car's paint finish as close as possible to the original condition—completely free of oxidation, stains, blemishes, bonded contaminants, and all other surface imperfections.

What It Does

In short, polishing will remove swirl

marks, light scratches and minor clear coat surface imperfections. It is a necessary step for (1) those with dark-colored cars whose desire is to have optimum gloss and depth of color; (2) those who apply products to their car

If the swirl marks and scratches are heavy, then you may use a buffer with a lighter pad for polishing. The frequency with which you polish depends on so many factors. Much depends on how well you maintain the finish, and how you store your car. Ultraviolet light, the main factor behind oxidation, is greatly reduced by frequent polishing. Photo by Jim Richardson

An orbital polisher is relatively safe. Its dual action will prevent it from burning through the paint. Orbitals are not very effective for deep cleaning paint, but sure do save a lot of time and effort. They also help to apply the product evenly.

of its impression into the paint. If it is more than minute, a cleaner and perhaps even a rotary buffer might be required. The key is to always use the least abrasive product possible to solve the problem—and avoid rubbing compounds if at all possible. After the use of a clearcoat safe cleaner, a pure polish will restore clarity and high gloss.

Orbital Polisher

The safest tool for polishing and waxing, for that matter, is an oscillating "orbital" polisher or a dual-action polisher. It is nearly impossible to burn paint with these types of machines because their rapid but limited movement does not generate any heat or abrasion. For this same reason, however, they are ineffective for correcting paint problems like stains, blemishes, oxidation and bonded contaminants. They are best suited for applying and removing polish and wax and the results they produce are on a par with a hand application. The big advantage they offer is increased speed with reduced effort without creating swirl marks, and that they apply the product in a more uniform manner.

The orbital polisher has a variety of pads available, ranging from terrycloth, foam and wool pads. Polishes and waxes are best applied with the terrycloth pad. For the final polishing of the wax coat and for swirl mark removal, special polyfoam pads are available.

There are polishing and wax products designed to work with an orbital polisher, and I can recommend them. With these, you'll only need to apply product to the pad. Applying it to the car surface is unnecessary. Squeeze out a generous portion of

will keep your car looking like new forever, because the oxidation process will never have a chance to begin.

In addition to keeping a paint healthy and vibrant, regular applications of a polish will restore and maintain clear reflection—which translates into high gloss.

Swirl Marks—Fine hairline scratches, often referred to as swirl marks, can destroy the appearance of paint that is otherwise healthy and vibrant. Each fine line impression refracts the light off in different directions, causing the reflection to be hazy and distorted under bright light. A pure polish has the ability to remove minute surface imperfections,

thereby restoring clearness of reflection and high gloss. The darker the color of the paint, the more pronounced these surface imperfections become. This is why a black car is so difficult to keep looking good when you are using the wrong products. And clearcoat finishes add to the problem because they are abrasion sensitive (they scratch very easily) and they actually magnify the appearance of every fine scratch. The good news is that it is easy to keep even a black car looking perfect when you use the right products. Keep in mind that the ability of a pure polish to remove a fine scratch depends entirely on the depth

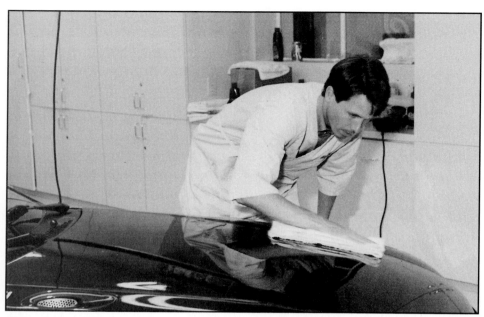

Although an orbital also can be used to remove wax or polish, many prefer a clean terrycloth towel. This gives you the opportunity to inspect the paint a bit more closely. Make sure you fold the towel often, and shake it out occasionally to release the dried polish buildup.

cleaner onto the terrycloth pad, work it into the pad, place the machine on the car's surface and pull the trigger.

Orbital polishers run at about 2000 to 6000 opm (oscillations per minute). With two hands on the machine, it is unlikely to get away from you because of its motion.

Technique—Move the machine around, spreading the product evenly over the surface. Start with the top of the car and do no more than a quarter of it at a time. Follow the product directions carefully. Every product is specifically designed to be applied a certain way. If you deviate, you'll get a less than satisfactory job.

Let the weight of the buffer do the job. Don't press down. Doing so will wear out the motor. When you get to the side (doors and fenders), you'll have to use your judgment about the amount of pressure to be applied. Let the product do the work, not your muscles. If the first application of cleaner seems not to do the job, try a second application or switch to a little more aggressive medium.

The orbital buffer will not generally burn through paint, with the possible exception of very thin areas around trunk lids, door edges and fender lips. Therefore, the pros will put masking tape over the edges of the trunk, hood and doors. The paint on the rounded edges of these areas is very thin. Mask them off; then, when the buffing is over, finish these areas by hand.

I recommend polishing the top of the vehicle first and then working your way down. It is not always necessary to wipe the vehicle down between the polishing and waxing procedure. However it is a great way to ensure that you have done a sufficient job polishing by allowing you to inspect the paint while wiping the paint down.

WAXING

A car wax is best described by characterizing its properties and uses. This is somewhat of an industry term, in that car waxes don't always, but most times do, contain wax. Just like

tin foil which does not contain tin and dish soap which does not contain soap, the technology has changed but the terminology has lagged behind. Car waxes are "finish products." Their purpose is to add durability to the finish, usually with emulsified silicone fluids and waxes, either in combination or individually.

Composition

Compounds, polishes, waxes and sealants are most commonly comprised of very tiny droplets (emulsion) of solvents, abrasives and active ingredients held in suspension in a water solution by emulsifiers. (Emulsifiers and emulsions can seem like mysterious concepts but actually are very common. Milk is an emulsion of milk fats and solids held in suspension by an emulsifier called casein.) A wax is different from the other products because it has less abrasive (powder) and the powder is very soft. Also the active ingredients are comprised of waxes, ordinary silicone fluids and/or polymers, in varying degrees and proportions. The combination of these light powders and active ingredients give the wax its depth, shine and moderate durability.

Benefits of Waxing

Protection is provided by creating an *ablative* (wears away slowly) surface between the expensive paint and the harsh environment. There are three main ways that this protection is provided:

1. Environmental fallout or acid rain and its associated particles are extremely corrosive to the paint surface. Waxes and silicones are formulated to repel and resist these contaminants.

CAUTION!

You should never use a wax or a product that contains any form of protection (like a polymer) on freshly re-painted cars, or areas that have been spot repainted, for at least 30 days, although 60 is recommended by most paint manufacturers. These are protection products which are formulated to seal the surface—and as such, they trap solvents in fresh paint and effectively stop the curing process. When this happens, fresh paint stays soft indefinitely and is highly susceptible to rapid degradation and abrasion. This is why protection products are only appropriate for cured finishes when your priority is long-lasting durability. Keep in mind that new car finishes are fully cured in high-temp ovens inside the assembly plants. As long as additional paint work has not been done, a new car finish is a cured finish that can be waxed immediately upon delivery. However, be aware that many dealerships apply spot repairs to fix any damage sustained during delivery of the vehicle.

There are waxes, and then there is carnauba. The wax made with pure carnauba will provide the best protection. Select as pure a grade as possible, and wax frequently.

2. Dirt and dust create an abrasive material on the paint surface that scratches the paint when touched. The damage caused by this stress is greatly reduced by improving the "mar and slip resistance" of the paint surface.

3. Oxygen in the atmosphere has an oxidizing effect on paint that is reduced by creating a barrier over the paint.

Durability

The best waxes tested last no more than two months or between 6 to 8 hand washes with a car wash soap, as opposed to a dish soap which is much too harsh. As stated before, waxes and polishes are designed to create an ablative surface. That is, they are supposed to wear away before the paint does but be less expensive and easier to apply than more paint.

Types of Waxes

Waxes form a broad category of organic (contain carbon) materials that don't fall into any one chemical family but are generally classed as lipids (for lack of a better place to put them). A material is called a wax if it:
• is solid at room temperature
• melts at a fairly low point (called thermoplastic)
• does not fall into the category of polymer.

The properties of waxes cover a large span of specifications but the "specs" that are important to automobile waxes are hardness, melting point, water repellency and resistance to breakdown by environmental factors.

There are many waxes available that fit the specs for a good automobile wax. They include vegetable waxes (carnauba), animal waxes (bees wax), mineral petroleum waxes (paraffin and microcrystaline), mineral fossil waxes (montan) and (despite the apparent contradiction) synthetic waxes (short chain ethylenic polymers).

The chemical formulas for these waxes are quite complex and diverse and not as important as the properties of the various grades.

There is no specific advantage of one wax over another (i.e. micro-crystaline wax is not intrinsically better than carnauba) because the waxes that are chosen for car waxes are all chosen for their properties that make them good for car waxes. A good wax for cars is fairly hard, melts at a reasonable temperature (not too

Wax is primarily for protection, and is formulated to wear in reaction to the elements (what is known as an ablative surface). A good wax for cars is one that is fairly hard, melts at a reasonable temperature, has good water repellency, and is difficult to apply. Therefore, most pros recommend that two thin coats of wax makes the best and easiest application, and that if you are going to wax as frequently as is recommended, you might want to invest in an orbital polisher, which is relatively inexpensive.

however, there is no residual value.

For those who do not have the time to polish their car on a regular basis, it is important to apply a protective coating on top of the paint finish. While car wax falls into this category of protection, there are a variety of other polymeric type materials that can give the appearance of your car added durability. Various waxes, polymers, silicones and resins each provide their unique resistance against various alkaline and acidic deposits, ultraviolet rays from the sun and the bonding of contaminants.

Applying Wax

Most pros agree that two thin coats of wax makes the best and easiest application. Although this is a step that can be done by hand, using an orbital buffer will not only make the job easier, it will also ensure that the wax is spread evenly. Select a top-of-the-line carnauba wax with the highest grade possible. Apply a large dollop of wax to the terrycloth pad on the orbital buffer or to a terrycloth hand towel folded to about a 1/2-inch thick. Apply this to a 2 to 3-foot square section of the car, starting with the roof and working downward. Repeat the process until you've covered the entire car. Remember not to overload the pad with product. Apply a thin, uniform layer.

When the wax has dried, get out a number of clean pads or towels. Using one of the towels or pads, begin buffing out the wax once it has dried to a dull haze. Use one pad or towel to remove the majority of the wax, then go over the car one last time with a fresh towel or pad to buff out the remaining wax. As you rub out the haze, replace the pad or towel with a clean one as soon as it begins to load

far from the boiling point of water), has good water repellency and will be darn tenacious stuff when you spread it out on a car. In fact many wax types can be blended together to further modify the properties of the finished product, gloss depth, durability.

One-Step Products

While you can never accomplish the same results with a one-step product that can be achieved by using three different products to clean, polish and protect, most people prefer a combination cleaner/wax product. The attraction, of course, is that they are simpler and easier to use. When doing so, however, keep in mind that a one-step product that will remove moderate to heavy contamination and

oxidation must, by necessity, be abrasive and therefore unable to create brilliant high gloss. Conversely, a one-step cleaner/wax that is capable of creating brilliant high gloss will be limited in its capacity to remove contaminants and oxidation. Applying a coat of protection to your car will slow down the oxidation process and make it more difficult for contaminants to bond to or etch into the finish. Applying a second or third coat of just wax (without cleaners or polish, which would remove the first coat), will provide even more protection and is something to consider each year before the harsh winter weather begins—particularly for the hood and below the beltline on the sides. After the third coat,

If this Saleen Mustang is going to keep this deep gloss, it will have to be maintained religiously. Using a quick, wipe on/wipe off product like Meguiar's Quik Detailer will help extend the time between polishing and waxing.

up with dried wax. Failure to keep using clean towels or pads will result in excessive swirl marks.

MAINTENANCE

Contrary to most of the car wax hype today, the easiest car care is regular car care. No matter what protection product you use, contaminants will continually land on your car's finish whenever it is outside. Some of these contaminants will begin to bond or etch into the finish almost immediately. This is why a regular routine of preventive maintenance is needed to counter their effects.

Once you have cleaned your paint finish and made it as smooth as glass, and then produced a durable high gloss finish by polishing and waxing it with carefully selected products, you can keep it looking like it was just detailed every day by following these simple steps:

• Whenever possible, park under cover
• When parking outside, use a car cover
• Use a spray quick detailer product regularly to remove contaminants when they are fresh, before they have time to bond or etch into the finish.
• Each time, after your car is washed, evaluate the finish by rubbing the top surfaces of your car with the face of your hand, allowing your sense of touch to tell you what your eyes cannot see. The finish should be as smooth as glass. Any and all contaminants that can be felt after washing should be removed with the non-abrasive clay described earlier.
• Dark colored cars should be re-polished whenever there is a loss of clarity, depth of color or gloss.
• To maintain optimum durability, a coat of protection should be re-applied: After the use of cleaners, clay

bars and polishes; when water becomes slow to wipe off; when water stops beading up on the surface; and when severe weather and/or road conditions are expected.

In spite of the over-proliferation of products in this category and the resulting mass of contradicting and exaggerated product performance claims, the task of restoring and maintaining a show car finish is really a simple one. Most importantly, common sense should prevail. Understand the basic steps of car care. Evaluate your finish to determine the correct type of products for your car. Buy those products from a manufacturer you can trust and from whom you can seek advice. Follow their directions and stay with a regular maintenance program. By so doing, I can assure you that you really will find it much easier to take home the trophy or to sell your car for top dollar.

49

5

EXTERIOR DETAILS

Vinyl tops and chrome trim should be treated with the same care and frequency as your paint. The true essence of detailing literally means to take care of little "details" such as these. Photo by Michael Lutfy

Cleaning and restoring painted surfaces is but one aspect of detailing. The paint can be in terrific shape, but if the chrome trim is a mess, then the paint job will not have as great an effect. Now you must take care of all those little "details" that are the true essence of detailing. This includes chrome, stainless and aluminum trim, weatherstripping, plastic door moldings and guards, and ancillary items like taillight lenses, headlights, and emblems. What about the trunk? This too must be dealt with, as should a convertible top.

It doesn't matter where you start on these exterior details, so let's start with the chrome trim, which includes bumpers, and bits of trim like that found around taillights and grille inserts. The chrome and stainless steel portions of this chapter are excerpted from Jim Richardson's *Tri-Five Chevy Handbook*, published by HPBooks.

RESTORING CHROME

No matter what else you do to your car, if its chrome is pitted and dull, your car won't impress anybody. Some older cars have miles of chrome, while today's cars have very little. Chrome is often used in strategic places like the grille, around the taillights and on the dash. Luckily for restorers, repro and restored parts are readily available if your car is missing some pieces, but of course, if your original trim is still pretty good, it is less expensive to have it replated most of the time. To ensure a successful job, follow these tips:

First, find a good plater. If possible, find a plater in your area that specializes in show chrome, or antique cars. Check some of the speed shops too. They often know who's hot and who's not. Also, attend the local car shows and ask the participants where they had their chrome done. The reason you want to find a shop

Chrome makes the difference between a show winner and an also ran. Here are some tips to help you take home the gold when you show your car.

that does more than just production work is because so much of a good plating job depends on the buffing and polishing of the metal underneath. A production shop is going to give you "good enough," not show-winning quality.

Two things can go wrong in the polishing stage. If the work isn't polished well enough, pits will still show, as will polishing marks. On the other hand, if the plater gets too aggressive with polishing, details such as lettering and small, decorative grooves can be buffed away. Another thing that sometimes happens at large volume production shops is they misplace some of your parts—and that can get expensive if they happen to be that rare set of fuelie flags for the front fenders of a '57 Bel Air or that Shelby Mustang emblem.

Remove your car's plated parts carefully so as not to tweak or break anything. There's actually a bit of an art form to it all. When you have them all off, lay them out on your garage floor and take a few pictures and make a checklist so you will be able to verify that nothing is missing when you get your parts back from the plater. Note any problems on your checklist as well, such as tears and pitting.

Support Chrome Strips

Tape long, thin or fragile strips of chrome to 1" x 3" pieces of wood prevent them from being bent accidentally, and to give the plater something with which to back the part while polishing it. Also, tape the threads of bolts that need plating with several layers of plastic electrical tape to keep them from being plated along with the bolt heads. If you don't do this, the bolts won't fit when you try to install them.

Repairing Severe Pits

It is probably not worthwhile to have severely pitted pieces replated, but if you have no choice with a rare part that you can't replace, you can have it copper plated, then take it home and silver-solder the pits. Make sure you use the correct silver solder as specified by your plater. Use a fine file to clean up your work, then take the part back to the plater to be polished and chromed.

Check for Nickel Shadow

When they are finished with your job and you pick up your parts at the chrome shop, unwrap and inspect each piece for nickel shadow before accepting it. Nickel shadow shows up

You won't want to take a rare emblem such as these fuelie flags to just any plater. To begin with, they might just lose them, and they may dissolve them if they aren't careful because they are made of pot metal which must be handled properly. Photo by Jim Richardson

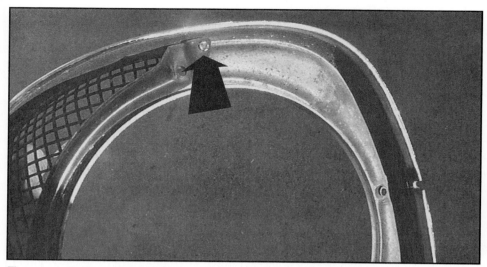

The screens in these '57 headlight eyebrows will need to be removed before plating the bezels. Photo by Jim Richardson

This light socket will have to come out too. If you don't do it, the plater will have to and you will be charged accordingly. Photo by Jim Richardson

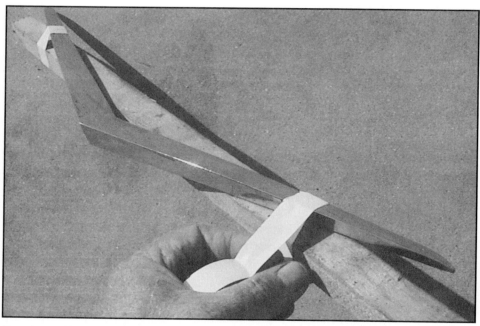

Tape long, thin or delicate items to strips of wood to keep them from getting kinked or bent. Photo by Jim Richardson

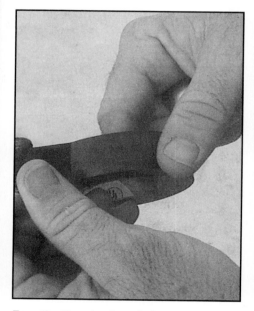

Tape the threads of any bolts such as these for the bumper with plastic electrician's tape to keep chrome off the threads. Chroming is an electro-chemical process. If the threads get plated, the nuts will not go back on. Photo by Jim Richardson

as a slight golden discoloration and indicates insufficient coverage of the chrome. If you are not sure, exhale on the part in question. Condensation from your breath will make nickel shadow more evident. If you find nickel shadow, peeling plating around the edges on bumpers, lines in the surface or rough spots, have the defective pieces redone.

Lay out all of your parts on the garage floor again when you get them home and make sure you have everything. Use your photos and checklist to verify that you got back what you sent out. At this point I like to give the backs of the bumpers and the unseen, undersides of other items a coat of epoxy primer, then shoot them with a couple of coats of silver, rust proof enamel to protect them. This is not show stock, but if you are going to drive your car at all, it will be good protection and is not likely to be spotted even by the fussiest judges.

Install Parts

To reinstall your chrome parts, use masking tape around painted panels liable to get bumped or scraped while

The Eastwood Co. kit for polishing stainless steel includes three buffing compounds, a sisal wheel, a sewn cotton wheel and an open polishing wheel. There is an expanding wheel and sanding belts, a special, stainless hammer and a small anvil available too. We'll be demonstrating on a '55 Chevy. Photo by Jim Richardson

When polishing chrome trim, make sure you use a specially formulated chrome polish. Chrome is a delicate coating, and a heavy abrasive will damage it. Photo by Jim Richardson

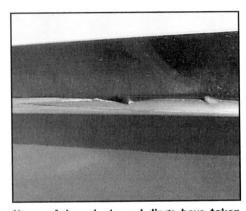

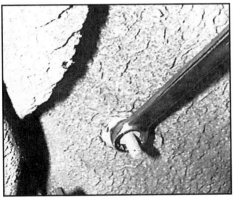

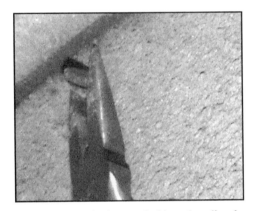

Years of door dents and dings have taken their toll, and the stainless trim on this car looks dull after forty years. Fortunately, making it look as good as new is easy. Photo by Jim Richardson

Long pieces of trim have bolts at their ends. Shoot them with a little penetrating oil, then loosen and remove the nuts holding them on. Photo by Jim Richardson

Long pieces of trim are held on by clips in most areas. Reach in with needle-nose pliers and squeeze the clips while a helper pulls gently from the outside. Photo by Jim Richardson

installing your bright work. Wax the paint that will be covered by trim several times before installing chrome pieces. Don't tighten fasteners so tight that you deform the parts or crack the paint underneath them.

Finally, always wax the chrome on your car. If you are storing it for the winter, add a heavy coat of wax and leave it on for the duration, buffing it when it emerges from hibernation. Never clean your chrome with abrasives such as household cleansers or waxes with abrasives in them. The layer of plating is very thin, even on

the best work, so just keep it clean and waxed. If you take care of it, your chrome work will make a show-winning impression for years to come.

Polishing Chrome

For maintenance, there are specially formulated chrome polishes available. Chrome is a very delicate plating, and can be rubbed off easily with scouring pads or heavy abrasives, so avoid these at all costs. Before polishing, make sure the chrome is clean, and don't use a heavy, stiff brush.

STAINLESS STEEL

Do you wish the stainless steel brightwork on your car looked as good as the trim on the cars you see at the shows? Well it can, and as it turns out, quite easily. First you will need to pick out the dents and dings, and then you will want to do a little filing, polishing and buffing to restore it to its former luster. That's all there is to it. And even if your trim has no dings, you'll be surprised what a little buffing will do to make it dazzling.

Have a helper support the trim and carefully pull it away. If you don't, it could scratch your paint when it comes loose. Photo by Jim Richardson

Pull up on wire retainers, then remove clips. Photo by Jim Richardson

Clean body hammers will do, but a special, small hammer for stainless work is ideal for taking out dents. Support your work with a small anvil or the heel of a vise. Photo by Jim Richardson

Start with 220 grit to remove pimples and high spots, then switch to #320, then #400 to remove scratches. Work back and forth in a criss-cross fashion to avoid deep grooves. Photo by Jim Richardson

Removal

Getting the trim off of your car without damaging your paint or breaking upholstery panels can be the toughest part of the job. A selection of tools for slipping in behind fasteners on upholstery is available at automotive tool stores and is a must for removing interior panels. Screwdrivers or putty knives aren't adequate for the job. If you are going

to replace the panels anyway though, the job is easy.

Work carefully, and squeeze the fasteners together from the inside while you pull gently with your fingers on the outside. Save the fasteners in plastic bags, and label the bags. Tape long, thin, stainless trim pieces to 1" x 3" strips of wood to avoid accidentally kinking or breaking them. Keep them taped to the wood while buffing the parts too.

Use one of the hammers specially

designed for working stainless such as the type that is available from The Eastwood Company to pick out the dings. Work from the outer edges to the centers of the dents to draw in the metal. Don't tap very hard, and use a small anvil, or the tail of a vise to back your work so you won't stretch the part and make more dents. Small, curved blocks of soft wood can also be used to tap dents to shape or to buck your work from the back.

Filing

Now use a fine file to carefully clean up any pimples. If you find small, low spots while filing, tap them out before going further. Only file enough to level the high spots. And be careful not to take off too much metal and weaken the part.

Sanding Stainless

Next, take out the file scratches using a rubber expanding wheel and #220 grit sandpaper. Work back and forth across the scratches so as not to make them worse. When the file marks are all gone, switch to #320-grit paper, then finish with #400 grit. Be sure to sand in a criss-cross fashion, moving the part back and forth, to minimize the scratches.

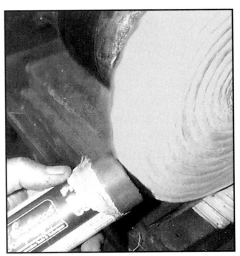

Switch to a sisal wheel for the heavy buffing to get the scratches out. Just use a little buffing compound. Don't clog the wheel. Photo by Jim Richardson

Next, clean the part with lacquer thinner to get the old compound off, then switch to the medium compound and a sewn, cotton wheel. Photo by Jim Richardson

Clean the part thoroughly again, let it cool, then finish with an open, cotton wheel and the white, polishing compound. Photo by Jim Richardson

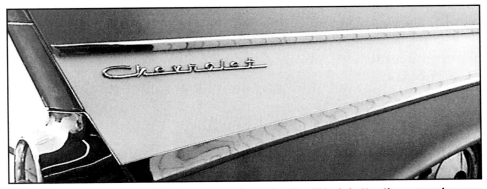

Use the open wheel to polish all of your stainless trim. It will look better than new when you are finished. Photo by Jim Richardson

Buffing Stainless

Now is the fun part. It is time to polish and buff your part to its original gloss. But before you begin, put on a face shield to protect your eyes from flying objects, leather gloves to protect your hands from injury, and a disposable particle mask to keep metal dust out of your lungs.

Use a sisal wheel and high speed buffer that turns at 3400 RPM to take out the sandpaper lines. Just briefly touch the wheel with a little heavy-duty compound made especially for buffing stainless, and then start moving the part lightly back and forth across the wheel, letting the spinning wheel—not pressure—do the work. Let the part cool after each buffing, then clean it carefully with lacquer thinner so you won't contaminate the next polishing wheel.

Next, go to a softer, sewn cotton wheel and emery compound and work at right angles to your previous polishing. Always hold your work below the wheel for safety's sake. Let the part cool again, then clean it and do the final buffing using jeweler's rouge or a specially formulated stainless steel polish, such as Flitz, Brasso, or those available from Mother's, Eagle One, or Turtle Wax, and an open, unsewn wheel. Store your buffing wheels separately in sealed plastic bags to avoid contaminating them with the wrong compound or dirt.

If you follow these simple tips, and work carefully, even old, dented and dull stainless can be made to look as good as when it came from the factory. You can pick up all the compounds and wheels you'll need to do this job in a kit from The Eastwood Company, The Eastwood Company 1-800-345-1178. FAX (610) 644-0560.

VINYL AND RUBBER

Dressing the exterior vinyl and rubber trim is somewhat of an art. The difference between slopping on dressing vs. dressing the exterior professionally to give the vehicle an overall natural dressed appearance is significant. The purpose of dressing is to restore the natural luster and shine to rubber, vinyl and plastic surfaces without making them look fake. The secret is to apply just enough product to restore them, not to cover them up. Moldings should look black and

A favorite spot for dirt and dried chrome polish is between the seams of the vinyl inserts on later model bumpers. A stiff bristle brush and a household or vinyl cleaner should be used first to remove the dirt.

Vinyl Trim Scuff Marks

Vinyl is frequently used as an insert on bumpers, and on door guards, and as such, it is often nicked and scratched. Most of these will be the result of parking lot bumps and careless door dings. There's a two-part solution to the problem.

Almost any mild rubbing compound will remove paint from vinyl without damaging it. The key word is mild. Don't use a heavy cutting compound. It's overkill. Vinyl and rubber release paint far more easily than another paint.

After compounding the abrasion, in most cases, this will be enough. If you still have an ugly looking surface, you can bring it right back with black vinyl paint. Any professional paint store serving the automotive community will carry aerosol cans of black vinyl paint. Buy a can of this, follow the directions on the label and recolor the damaged area. Just remember to clean the vinyl first with a good grade of silicone and wax remover. I like Rinshed-Mason products for this application. Be sure you mask off anything on which you do not want overspray. Don't try to spot repair the area. These are usually very obvious. Instead, refinish the entire piece of vinyl.

SEALS & WEATHERSTRIPPING

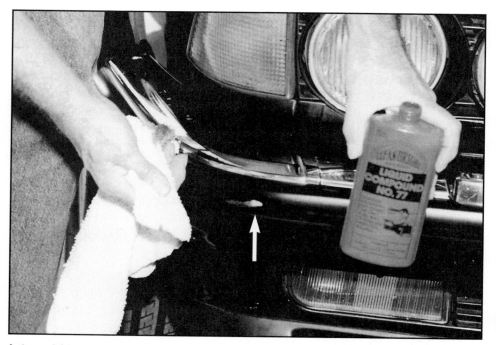

Late-model bumpers with vinyl inserts are magnets for scuff marks. These can often be buffed out by hand with a mild to medium cleaner or polishing compound. Follow up by using a vinyl protectant after buffing.

natural but not overly glossy.

To do moldings and rubber trim, P&S Sales makes a product called Multi Dressing that cleans and protects with one step, and works equally as well on rubber as on vinyl.

Eagle One and Meguiar's, as well as Turtle Wax and Armorall, make a similar dressing. Whichever you choose, apply the dressing first to a towel, then wipe on, applying dressing frequently.

Weatherstripping and seals, like those around the trunk and doors, are often overlooked. Check them carefully to be sure they are not cracked, torn, or broken. Long, deep cracks are not acceptable. When this occurs the rubber should be replaced. Small breaks and tears may be

A small crack like this one may be possible to repair. 3M's Weatherstrip Adhesive is an excellent product for this type of repair. If you are trying to locate weatherstripping for a classic car, A&M Soffseal has replacements for many different types of classic and collectible cars. Their address and phone can be found in the classifieds of many automotive enthusiast publications.

Westley's Bleche-Wite is very good at cleaning rubber weatherstripping. There are some weatherstrip cleaners specially formulated for this task, but this product, which I need for my tires anyway, does an excellent job.

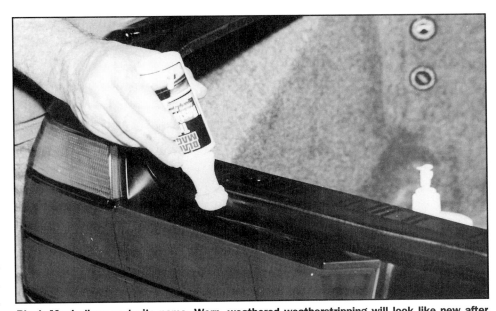

Black Magic lives up to its name. Worn, weathered weatherstripping will look like new after one application.

cemented back together with 3M Weatherstrip Adhesive. 3M Weatherstrip Adhesive comes in two colors, black and yellow. Yellow is the strongest but, of course, doesn't blend with the black rubber. Select the black adhesive for this project.

Restoring Weatherstripping

There are vinyl and rubber cleaners/condtioners, and a few available for weatherstripping. I prefer *Westley's Bleche-Wite*, the same stuff used to clean whitewalls, to clean weatherstrip.

For restoring that deep, black look, I like *Black Magic Trim Restoration* to dress the rubber seal. The nice thing about this product is twofold: the bottle has an applicator (much like a shoe polish applicator which makes applying the product a snap) and,

when dry, the seal will not stick to the metal of the trunk lid or door. There are several products that will do this, but this one works best for me.

PLASTIC TRIM & LIGHTS

These include taillight lenses, medallions and logos, and other plastic trim. Meguiar's Clear Plastic Cleaner/Polish, which is specially formulated for the rear windows on convertible tops, also does a great job on other plastics than just clear. If you use this product, be careful not to get it on the paint. Apply it with a towel,

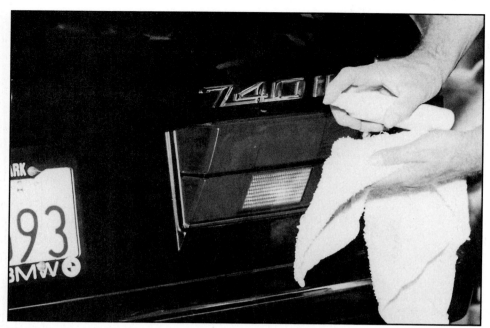

Meguiar's Clear Plastic Cleaner works very well on taillight lenses.

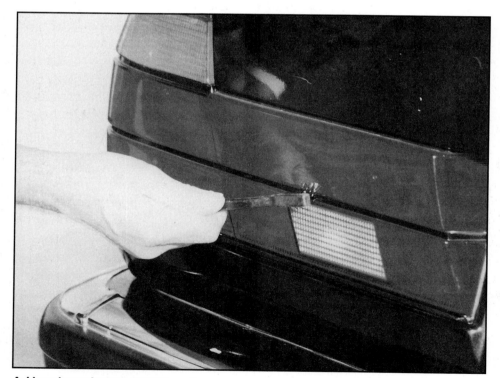

Acid swabs work great on tight crevices.

as you wash the car, but a detailer goes beyond this. After washing, you can use a glass cleaner, or glass polish on the windows. From Windex™ to specialty products developed by aftermarket manufacturers, all work equally as well.

One very irritating aspect to cleaning the windows is the overspray that inevitably occurs. I like to use a little contraption commonly sold in supermarkets that is a small sponge with a hollow handle attached to it that serves as a soap dispenser (see the photo nearby). With this unit, you can apply cleaner and scrub it off, then buff the excess with a clean towel.

This brings up another point: there are many people who swear by newspaper as the ultimate window buffing tool, and I'm one of them. Others advocate two towels, or a squeegee followed by a towel. It really is a matter of personal preference.

If you are driving a collectible car, chances are you would be horrified to get stuck in the rain, but sometimes it is unavoidable. One product that I can recommend is Rain-X, which effectively acts as an "invisible windshield wiper." It also improves visibility.

Chips & Scratches

Two very common problems with windshields on older vehicles are minor stone chips which just seem to naturally occur with use, and "wiper haze": those annoying small scratches on the windshield where the wipers travel. The Eastwood Company has two methods for repairing these irritating problems that you can perform in your own garage. We'll cover chip repair first:

Chip Repair—Picture this scenario:

and buff off when wet. Better yet, remove the tailllight lens or trim piece if possible to get it thoroughly clean.

With medallions, small emblems and tiny trim pieces, try using cotton swabs to apply the product. These

items keep the plastic polish off the paint in a way no other tool can.

WINDOWS

Washing windows should be done

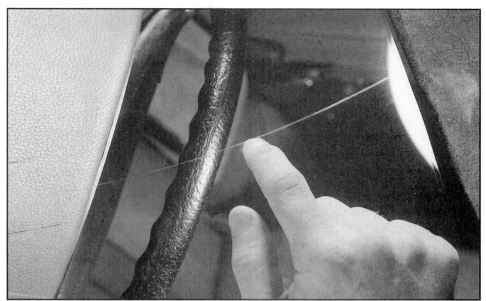

The Eastwood Co. (610/640-1450) offers a glass polishing kit that can remove minor windshield scratches. To see if a scratch is light enough to be buffed out, run your fingernail across the scratch. If your fingernail does not get caught in the scratch and can pass over it, then the windshield can be polished. Photo courtesy The Eastwood Co.

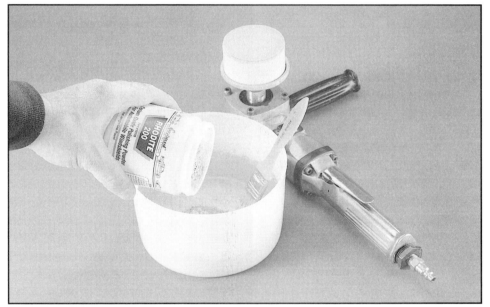

The windshield polishing kit contains the compound, a special felt buffing pad, which works with an electric drill or a low-speed polisher. Mix the compound according to the directions. Photo courtesy The Eastwood Co.

With an erasable marker, trace the scratch from the inside of the windshield to act as a guide. Photo courtesy The Eastwood Co.

It is a beautiful weekend afternoon, the sun is shining and you are taking your very special vehicle out for a spin. Driving along a winding country road, following a car ahead of you and then you hear it: CHINK! A small stone has hit your windshield. You pull over to assess the damage and there it is: a small, bullseye chip out of the glass. Now you have three options: the first is to replace the windshield (very expensive and on some rare vehicles, nearly impossible), a trip to the glass repair shop (also expensive and time-consuming as well), or repair the minor damage yourself using Eastwood's Windshield Repair Kit. This kit allows you to repair these bullseye type chips yourself, saving both time and money. This kit uses the same type of materials a pro glass shop uses: a pro quality injector and permanent, crystal-clear resin. Using the included components, the resin is actually forced into the damaged area, bonding permanently with the glass to form a virtually undetectable repair. To make the best use of the Windshield Repair Kit, I recommend using Eastwood's Diamond Windshield Burr which very thoroughly cleans out the bullseye chip and evens its edges, allowing the Repair Kit's resin to better hold on to the good glass in the windshield.

Slight Scratches—After years of use, many car windshields get scratched by the windshield wipers. These light scratches are sometimes called "wiper haze." Before Eastwood made its glass polishing kit available, the only way to fix this relatively minor damage was to replace the windshield. Now, using Eastwood's Pro Glass Polishing Kit and a little time, you can restore your windshield

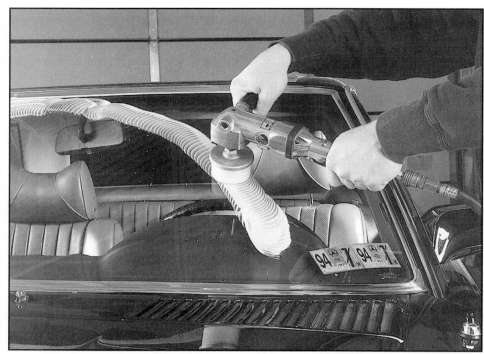

Using light pressure, buff along the scratch, allowing it to overlap. Repeat as necessary. Wipe off with a towel. Photo courtesy The Eastwood Co.

Most convertible tops are made of two types of fabric: Haartz or Cambria cloth and vinyl. For the cloth types, use an interior cloth seat cleaner, or upholstery cleaner. Dilute the solution about 4 parts water to 1 part cleaner. Try not to use a brush, but if you need to for heavy soiling, then use a soft bristled one as shown above.

to like-new condition.

The first step is to determine if your windshield can be polished. To find this out, do this simple test: just run your fingernail across the damaged area. If your fingernail does not get caught in the scratch and passes right over it, then your windshield can be polished. If your fingernail does get

caught, then the scratch is too deep to be removed by polishing. Most windshields usually pass this test.

Using the kit is simple. Just mark the damaged area of the windshield on the inside of the glass. Then mix the special polishing compound with water, apply to the windshield and buff with the special felt buff using

your electric drill or low-speed polisher. Your windshield will be looking brand-new in no time!

CONVERTIBLE TOPS

You might think convertible tops are a no-brainer, but they really aren't. Convertible tops are either made of cloth (high end) or vinyl (everyone else). Most convertible tops today have a glass rear window, but there are still quite a few with a plastic window. Both types of tops require different approaches in care.

Fabric Tops

There are two types of cloth used in convertible tops today: Haartz cloth and Cambria. Both of these incorporate two layers of cloth, very similar to a light canvas. Sandwiched between these is a layer of rubber film. This is the real water barrier. The best care that can be given to either of these two brands of cloth is to keep them clean and out of the weather as much as practical.

The first step is to wash the top. However, do not use the same car wash soap solution you used on the paint. Although mild, it is still too strong for the cloth top. Instead, use a diluted solution of an interior seat cloth cleaner, like those offered by Eagle One, Meguiar's or Mother's. The dilution should range anywhere from 4 parts to 8 parts of water to one part cleaner, depending on how dirty the top is. If the top is fairly clean, use the weaker solution. If the top has heavy soiling, grime, or spots, use the stronger mix. If there is very heavy soiling, use the solution straight. When this is necessary, spray a little onto a clean terrycloth towel and work one 2x2 foot section at a time. This

Rinse thoroughly, and wipe off with a dry, clean terrycloth towel. If you find any spots, spot-clean by applying cleaner to the towel.

Vinyl tops, like the one on this late-model Mustang, should first be cleaned with a vinyl or a leather cleaner. If there is mildew present, scrub it down first with a solution of 4 parts water to 1 part ammonia to kill the mildew. Make sure you don't use household cleaners on vinyl, however.

Squirt enough of the diluted solution to build a good sudsing, and scrub with a cotton towel. Try not to use a brush, but if you must, make sure it is a soft bristle.

If the top has a clear vinyl rear window, avoid getting any of the cleaning solution on it, and if you do, rinse it off before it dries, and do not scrub it with anything abrasive, sponge or otherwise. It is very susceptible to scratches.

When the top has been thoroughly scrubbed, rinse with a strong spray of water to get the cleaning solution out of the top. It's needed to get the solution out from between, in, and under the treads of the top. Even after the water runs clean continue for a minute or two more, just to make sure all of the cleaning solution is out. It's much like trying to get all of the soap out of a sponge. Dry the top with a man-made chamois.

VINYL TOPS

Cleaning colored vinyl is quite a bit different than cleaning clear vinyl, and vinyl tops in general require specific care. According to Roger Dyer, of 303 Products, a company known for its specialized protective coatings, the problem is ultra-violet light. Before UV light can cause damage, it must be absorbed. If it is not turned into heat or transferred to a nearby stabilizer molecule called a "quencher," it breaks weak chemical bonds, and that's just the beginning of damage to your car's vinyl. If the absorbers are not stabilized, discoloration, drying, fading and cracking will occur eventually.

The process is not unlike what happens to your skin. You would add a sunscreen to prevent absorption of

prevents getting excess cleaner on the top where it's not needed.

Washing—Test the colorfastness of the top by rubbing a small amount on an obscure corner to check. I'm assuming that you are also washing the entire car at the same time, so before you lather up the convertible top, apply a heavy layer of suds to the painted surface of the car. The interior cleaner that will drain from the top may strip the wax, and a heavy layer of suds will prevent this. Of course, if your detailing plans include adding a coat of wax after the wash, then this step is not necessary.

CONVERTIBLE TOP DOS & DON'TS

• After washing, make sure that the top is completely dry before lowering to avoid water stains on interior materials and mildew damage to the rear window.

• Mildew may occur more rapidly if the top remains lowered for extended periods of time under damp conditions. Mildew appears brownish in color and may give off an undesirable odor. No amount of cleaning can reverse this condition. If it occurs, the window must be replaced.

• Do not use brushes and automatic car washes, as they may abrade the rear window, top material and threads.

• Do not use a dry cloth to remove even the slightest amount of dust from a plastic rear window. Use a soft cotton towel saturated with water and gently wipe in a horizontal and vertical direction.

• Do not use a scraper, de-icing chemicals or sprays to remove frost, snow, or ice from the window. In an emergency, warm water (never hot) may be used. Hot water may cause permanent warping or shrinking of the window material.

• Do not use solvents, such as: alcohol, nail polish remover, or paint thinner on the back window or top.

• Do not use bleach, ammonia, window cleaner, or all-purpose household cleaners on the rear window or the top.

• Do not use surface protectants, cleaners, polishes, waxes, so-called "beautifiers", or any compound or solution containing silicone.

• Do not apply advertising stickers, gummed labels, or adhesive tape to the window. Such items will damage the rear window.

---

ultraviolet light, which is basically what is recommended with vinyl tops. The UV stabilizers have to be periodically renewed or replenished to provide lasting protection. There is no such thing as a "permanent" protectant, just as there is no permanent sunscreen for your skin.

Washing

Chad Heath of Eagle One recommends using leather cleaner on the vinyl roof. Just be sure you don't use household cleaners, powdered or other abrasives, steel wool, industrial cleaners, dry cleaning fluids, solvents, bleach or detergents. Use a medium soft brush, warm soapy water (with car wash soap or dish soap, in this case), rinse with cool water, then dry with a chamois. All of this should take place in the shade.

Mildew—Mildew is particularly prevalent on vinyl tops. You must kill the mildew before it takes hold. Use a medium soft brush and vigorously brush the area with a mixture of 4 to 1, water to ammonia, then rinse. If the stains are really tough, try a solution of 1 teaspoon of ammonia, 1 cup of hydrogen peroxide and three quarters cup of distilled water. All cleaning must be followed with a very thorough rinse.

If the top needs two applications of cleaner, set the car in the shade with the cleaning solution on the top and let it soak for a while. This will help loosen the dirt. Keep the top wet with further applications of cleaner or mist with water.

Protectant

There are many other types of vinyl solutions available, but generally, buy one that specifically offers a UV protective coating.

Make sure that you buff with a clean towel before the protectant dries. Apply with one towel, buff with another.

There are many vinyl conditioners available, and some tire dressings will work just fine as well. But the biggest enemy of vinyl is ultraviolet light. Make sure you get a product that is formulated with UV protection. Buff well, and apply several coats.

PLASTIC REAR WINDOWS

Perhaps as many as half the tops in existence today have clear vinyl rear windows. These clear vinyl windows are extremely susceptible to ultraviolet light, acid rain, smog and will scratch with a fingernail. These windows often succumb to these elements and develop a fog or haze. This condition can be prevented by frequent and regular maintenance, but if that is not the case, minor hazing and fogging can be repaired.

If the deterioration, hazing, or fogging is still in the gray looking stage, most of that can be removed. Some of it may have turned a light to dark brown. If this is the case, it's beyond repair. Light brown "stains" are not stains. Rather, they're burns; and, the darker the brown, the deeper and harsher is the burn. If your window is burned, replace it and keep it maintained.

Washing

The first step is to get the window clean. Wash the rear window using gentle horizontal and vertical strokes—do not use a circular motion. Use a clean terry towel if dirt and grit has accumulated in the first towel.

Rinse with clean water. Make sure all detergent is flushed off the body. Do not allow soap solution or rinse water to dry on the finish or the rear window, it will cause streaking.

Use a clean damp terry cloth towel and gentle pressure to remove the majority of the rinse water allowing the remaining water film to air dry. Replace the towel frequently to avoid scratches from entrapped dirt.

Removing Haze & Scratches

Meguiar's makes a fantastic plastic cleaner and a plastic polish, a two-step process that I personally favor. Eagle One has an all in one product that works well.

Apply the cleaner with a terrycloth towel or diaper, rub vigorously using horizontal and vertical strokes—do not use a circular motion. Allow the cleaner to dry to a haze, then buff off with a separate towel, using the same vertical/horizontal stroke direction. Do the inside as well, and make sure there is no grit on the towels. This will instantly scour the soft window surface.

You should apply the polish or protectant on the rear window a minimum of every 30 days.

Meguiar's has a two-step cleaner and polish system to remove light scratches and haze from plastic rear windows. When applying, use one towel to apply, one to buff off. Use vertical and horizontal strokes, rather than a circular motion. Make sure you do the inside as well, and polish the window frequently to keep it looking new. Photo by Michael Lutfy

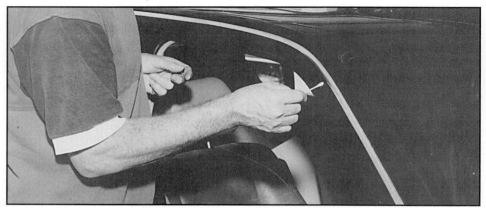

To ensure you don't get vinyl trim restorer or protectant on your paint, you need a greater measure of control for the edges. That's where these cotton swabs come in.

Dirt, grime and wax build up in the crevice around the door lock. Use a toothpick to dig it out, and then use one wrapped in cotton and dipped in a household cleaner such as Fantastik or 409 to clean it.

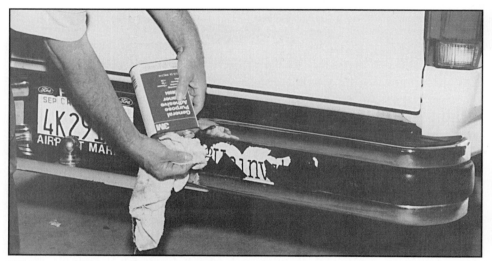

Old bumper stickers are best removed with 3M's General Purpose Adhesive Remover. Peel off as much of the sticker as possible. Wet a towel with the remover, then rub on and watch it work.

For windows, this dish soap dispenser sponge tool, available in many supermarkets, works wonderfully as an applicator for glass cleaning solution. This will prevent overspray from getting on your paint.

Black Satin is formulated specifically for repainting metal trim parts. Black trim strips deteriorate easily. The black fades and the strips are chipped. Mask off the area, sand, clean and shoot on this trim coating. This is one more of those "exterior details" you can't afford to overlook. Photo by John Pfanstiehl

No vehicle is complete without a fine looking set of wheels and tires. Keeping them clean and polished is a challenge, but no less important than any other area of the car. Photo by Michael Lutfy

6

WHEELS & TIRES

What can be more beautiful than a good looking set of wheels and tires on a sharp car? We're so infatuated with our wheels that very often we'll go out and buy the set we've dreamed about before we get around to painting the car. How many times (each day) do you see that old Camaro, Firebird or Mustang driving down the street with fine chrome or "mag" wheels, big wides in the back, and rust beginning to poke through the primer? The rest of the car may be going to hell, but not the wheels and tires. Custom wheels are much like jewelry, and about as expensive. It is not uncommon for one tire and wheel combination to exceed $1200 or more. Multiply that by four, and you have a substantial investment in these things. Furthermore, many classic cars, especially pre-war, are shod with irreplaceable rims. Both of these are strong arguments for deep cleaning, polishing and protecting your wheels.

If you're detailing the entire car at once, then the tires and wheels should have been washed during the overall washing process of the car. However, you may find that you'll need to wash, clean and polish the tires and wheels more frequently than the rest of the body. They are, after all, on the front lines between the pavement and your car, and take quite a beating from road grime, brake dust and tar.

PROCEDURE

Previous chapters have hammered home the concept of "wash, clean, polish, protect," and tires and wheels are no different. Washing in this sense is with detergent, then you'll clean with a wheel or tire cleaner, polish them, then add a protectant.

When you wash the wheels, do all

A good procedure to follow is to wash the wheels and tires, deep clean the wheel, deep clean the tire, dress the tire, then polish the wheel. Photo by John Pfanstiehl

four one after another, at the same time. The folks at Enviro-Clean recommend that you break the cleaning process down into smaller steps. Example: clean the right rear wheel rim and tire, clean the right front wheel well, rim and tire, clean the left rear wheel well, rim and tire, clean the left front wheel well, rim and tire, and then rinse all wheel wells, rims and tires at the same time. This will help in simplifying the overall procedure.

However, there are a number of opinions as to the order of things after that. Should the tire or wheel be detailed next? Opinions and preferences for each differ from detailer to detailer, but my suggestion is to deep clean the wheel first, then clean the tire, polish and protect the tire, then polish and protect the wheel. This way, any run-off from the tire can be polished off of the wheel at the end.

Whichever one you do first, the pros recommend that you detail one wheel and tire combination at a time after

washing. This prevents cleaner from drying on the wheel or tire—a condition which may leave a stain. So although you'll be hosing everything off at the start, clean and detail each set before moving to the next one.

If you have driven the car, make sure you let the tires and wheels cool down. Road friction and braking will have heated them up quickly, and some of the compounds we'll be using can work too aggressively when heated. This could cause etching—especially with mag wheels and anodized aluminum. So give the car time to cool down and heavily rinse the wheels before you begin washing.

PAINTED WHEELS

Many cars on the road and in garages today have painted wheels, especially classics. The wheel generally has a hubcap—either a small center cap, full wheel cover, or beauty rim. If your car has this arrangement, begin by removing anything that comes off. Be careful in

the doing. Avoid prying them off with a screwdriver if there's any chance of scratching the wheel paint. A small block of wood used as a fulcrum will let you pry off most anything without scratching your paint.

If you still tend to worry about scratching, go to your local hardware store and buy a can of liquid plastic. This is the stuff you dip your pliers handles into to give them a better grip. Select an old screwdriver you would probably be throwing away and dip the blade into the liquid plastic. Allow it to dry. Now, you can use this to do some serious prying without scratching the wheel paint. With the hubcap, wheel cover, or beauty rim off, it's time to get them seriously clean.

Hubcaps

Begin with the hubcap if the wheel has one. Remove the cap and hose it down to get off any loose grime, both front and back, then thoroughly wash the cap on both sides. The reason: the back side of the hubcap collects as much, or more, dirt than the outside, especially if the back side of the cap has never been washed. There will probably be a large amount of metallic brake dust and bearing grease. Suppose you left the cap on the wheel, washed it there, then wiped it dry? In two or three minutes a great streak of dirty water will come pouring over your newly cleaned wheel and tire. Check out some wide whitewall tires and look for the telltale stain of dirty water running out of the inside of the cap. Avoid this by washing the backside of your hubcap.

Plain soap (dishwashing liquid) and water will be all you need for most hubcaps. If, however, you happen to have disc brakes, you might be better

Many cars still have painted wheels. The paint is generally the same type as used on the body. The techniques used to detail these wheels are the same ones used to detail a body panel.

body. Begin with an analysis of the condition. Should they be repainted or will a little touch-up paint cover the nicks and scratches? Let's start with just a little touch-up.

Touch-Up Painting—Three areas of the wheel are subject to scratching: the ridge upon which the hubcap clamps; the groove wherein they attach the wheel weights; and the very outside edge. Touch-up paint for these areas is available in two locations. If the wheels are from a fairly late-model vehicle, you can buy a two-ounce bottle of touch-up paint (with applicator) from the dealer. If the dealer has discontinued the line, you'll have to go to your local paint-supply house. First, however, you'll need the paint code.

The easiest way to do this is to find your VIN (Vehicle Identification Number) number, copy it down, and take it with you to the paint shop. Most late-model cars have the VIN number attached to the instrument panel on the driver's side, next to the

off using one of the specialized wheel cleaners. Eagle One, Meguiar's and Mother's make a number of wheel cleaners, specific to the metal they will clean: aluminum, chrome, stainless and magnesium. Select the least aggressive of these cleaners to do the job. The hubcap demonstrated is made of stainless steel. However, part of it was painted. Therefore, we used a cleaner that would not affect the paint.

When the hubcap is clean and dry, you must bring it up to its best possible appearance and condition. If part of it is painted, repaint that area. Mask off everything but the painted surface, then go after it with an appropriate paint. If there are any plastic medallions, refer to page 57 and follow the directions for cleaning and polishing plastic. When the hubcaps are perfect, set them aside and turn your attention to the wheels.

Wheel Surface

Painted wheels must be treated just like a painted body. You washed them with the same cleaning solution. Now, they must be detailed the same as the

The wheel may have been painted a custom color. If it needs touch-up paint, you'll have to have some custom paint mixed at a specialty paint shop. The paint touch-up procedures are similar to those on pages 40-43. The wheel paint can then be maintained with polish and wax, using the products and techniques used to detail the car's painted surfaces.

If the wheel needs a complete repaint, unmount the tire, then have the wheel sandblasted. Shoot it with primer, paint and clearcoat, then color sand, polish and wax—just as you would with a body panel.

windshield. Some have it on the door jamb. From this number the counterperson can determine the paint code and mix up a half-pint of the correct color.

If, however, your car has been repainted a custom color, you're going to have to go for an "eye match." The paint-supply house will mix a quart of paint to match your existing color—exactly. With paint in hand you're ready to begin. To repair paint chips, the technique is the same as demonstrated on page 40 of this book.

Here's a nifty trick to save time and money. Instead of buying a touch-up brush (which must be cleaned), use the fuzzy end of a paper match, torn from a book of matches. This can then be thrown away when you're finished. I think this does a better job than the brush. If your analysis says the wheels must be repainted, then there are two approaches you can take.

Full-Painting—If the wheels are chipped, scoured, nicked and the paint is peeling, then you'll need to fully repaint them. The first step is to have them sandblasted, or chemically stripped to have all paint removed. Then you'll need to paint them using the paint techniques illustrated in HPBooks' *Paint & Body Handbook.* It's a bit beyond the scope of this book to cover primer, top coats, spray guns, clearcoat, etc., so if you're not already familiar with these techniques, then pick up a copy of that book.

There are two ways to approach the problem of painting the wheels: tires mounted to the wheel with the wheel on the car, or, tires off the wheel and the wheel off the car. The latter, by far, is the best way—albeit, the most expensive and time consuming.

The downside is having them remounted without undoing all of your hard work. A standard tire shop

chain most likely will not care as much about your classic, hand-painted wheels as you do. If you can find one in your area, go to an automotive restoration shop, one used to handling classic, irreplaceable items, and either have them do it (if they are capable), or ask for a recommendation.

Once the wheels are painted, they can be polished.

Deep Cleaning and Polishing Painted Wheels

There are wheel cleaning products available that are specifically formulated for painted wheels. If you can't find one, choose a cleaner that is either the least powerful or designed as a general purpose cleaner. Use a nylon bristle brush or your cut-off paint brush to get into all the cracks and crevices. In fact, if you want to do the super job, take the wheel off the drum and deep clean the back! This is a "must" situation if you're detailing a show car.

Spray the cleaner all over the wheel and let it set for five or 10 minutes. This will loosen all the grime. Next, get into every crevice with your brush. Finally, rinse the wheel thoroughly. I like to continue using my brush on the wheel while rinsing. This just gets more of the loose dirt off. As I stated before, you can't rinse too much. When the wheel is as clean as it can be, the next step is to jump ahead and clean the tire, then polish or wax the wheel. This is so you'll remove any overspray from the tire before polishing the wheel. Painted wheels and hubcaps need to be treated like any other painted surface to restore gloss and add protection—by using polish and wax.

Specialty wheels need custom care. The key is to match the properly formulated cleaner and polish to the wheel type. Photo by Michael Lutfy

SPECIALTY WHEELS

Specialty wheels encompass all wheels that are more than just a painted wheel with a hubcap, although you'll find many specialty custom wheels that have painted centers with a small hub cap, and these painted areas should be treated as previously described. Typically, you'll find specialty wheels made of chrome, stainless steel, magnesium, aluminum, and anodized aluminum.

Wheel Cleaners

Many wheel cleaners are specially formulated for a specific type of surface, and there are some that can work on several surfaces. Use a cleaner that contains no acid, toxins or abrasives first. If it is ineffective, move on to something stronger. Meguiar's, Mother's and Eagle One all offer excellent wheel cleaners that meet these criteria. But remember: with metal wheels, it is very critical that you match the cleaner to the material. It is especially important not to clean aluminum with a magnesium cleaner. Magnesium cleaners have a slightly caustic base that will stain some types of aluminum. Use care and caution. A mag wheel cleaner is much too aggressive to be used on aluminum—and especially on anodized aluminum. Look hard for a specific cleaner. You'll get the best results with this. If you can't find that specific cleaner, buy a good generic cleaner from a known brand such as Eagle One's ALL WHEELS Brake Dust Cleaner.

Cleaning & Polishing

Begin the process by determining exactly what type of wheel you have. If you don't know, go to the auto dealer for your brand of car, or to a specialty custom wheel shop. You need this information, because some wheels are not what they seem. An aluminum wheel can be cast aluminum, cast aluminum with a machined or polished edge, coated or anodized aluminum, uncoated aluminum or fully-polished aluminum, or even chromed aluminum. It gets even deeper. How about chromed steel wheels, chromed wheels with painted or clearcoat areas, true wire wheels (chromed or stainless steel

Fortunately, manufacturers like Eagle One and Mother's offer a variety of wheel specific cleaners.

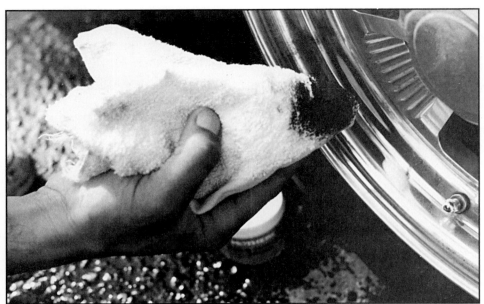

Check to see if the wheel is clearcoated by applying polish to a small area of the rim. If you don't see black as shown above, that means your wheel has a clearcoated finish, and you'll need to get a cleaner and polish specially formulated for this. This is a non-clearcoated, polished aluminum wheel. Photo courtesy Mother's.

damaged. Use a very mild cleaner for this type of wheel. Follow it with an ultrafine polishing compound. Avoid any hard rubbing as this will polish out the brushing, returning the aluminum to its original polished condition. Should you find a previous owner has polished away the brushing, it can be restored. Very fine steel wool or an ultra fine Scotchbrite pad soaked in WD-40 and applied with a bit of "elbow grease" will restore the brushed surface better than the old "eraser method." Next, finish it with a light coat of good wax.

Non-Coated, Polished Cast Aluminum—Unless your cast aluminum wheels are new or have been well maintained, it's most likely you will have some kind of pitting problem. This is a result of acid residue from the pavement, and little stones and road debris, which can literally sandblast the surface. However, these wheels can be brought back to a new appearance if you're willing to put in the work, as long as

spokes), or "wire basket" hubcaps? The list is endless. So find out what you have before you use a cleaner that could harm the surface. One little tip: to determine if your polished aluminum wheel is clear coated or not, look at the wheel in a bright light. If you see a prism-like effect (a rainbow hue of colors) then the wheel is probably clear coated. Another method is to take a polish, such as Mother's Mag & Aluminum polish, and rub it on a small area of the rim. If you *do not* get black residue immediately, STOP! Your wheel is clear coated and you will have to use a different, clear coat safe cleaner, most likely something that sprays on and rinses off without hard rubbing. You don't want to rub off the clear coat.

You should use the least aggressive cleaning product available. So, when you determine what the composition of your wheel is, get a cleaner for the most sensitive part of the wheel, as well as a corresponding polish.

Brushed Aluminum—Brushed aluminum looks as if you had rubbed an eraser over the surface of a shiny piece of aluminum. Back in the fifties we called it "burnished" aluminum. Now it's simply "brushed."

This type of surface is easily

If you can't determine the exact wheel type, or don't want to take the time, get an all-purpose cleaner like this one from Mother's. Spray on liberally, and use a soft brush to agitate any stubborn spots. Photo courtesy Mother's.

The instructions for this Mother's All-Purpose Wheel Cleaner said to allow the cleaner to soak for a few minutes, then rinse off. Most other cleaners are similar, but check the directions to make sure. Photo courtesy Mother's.

should never have to go to the steel wool step again.

Painted and Anodized Aluminum—Anodizing is a process of adding a protective oxide coating to a metal surface by using the metal as the anode in an electrical cell and allowing an electrolyte to act on it. Often, a coloring agent will be added to the coating, but because the coating is clear, the brilliance of the aluminum still shines through. This type of surface should be handled with the most delicate of touches and the least abrasive materials possible, as it can easily be worn away. If you wear it away, short of having it anodized again, there's no way to restore it to its original look. So handle with care.

Painted and anodized aluminum wheels should be treated in the same way we earlier discussed painted steel wheels. Use a cleaner specific to painted wheels and go easy with the scrubbing. Use a soft to medium nylon bristle brush with patience

they are not clear coated.

Begin cleaning with a good aluminum wheel cleaner. Because you're working with cast aluminum (solid aluminum all the way through with no surface texturing) there is little you can do to damage it. Anything you do will improve the appearance.

To get rid of that pitting you must work the surface down with progressively finer polishing compounds. Begin with fine steel wool, grade 00, used with more of your aluminum wheel cleaner. When the surface has been fully covered with this level of cleaning, go to a finer steel wool such as a grade 0000. Steel wool comes in grades as fine as 000000. When all of the pitting is gone, turn to a good rubbing compound followed by a very fine polish. By then your wheel will look like new. Your arm and hand, however, will probably feel like they're ready to fall from their sockets. A little muscular soreness is a

small price to pay to restore a set of wheels whose replacement cost could be several hundred dollars.

As before, follow up with a good wax. With a consistent, regular polishing and waxing routine, you

Use a clean towel and rub a small section of the wheel in a circular motion. Polish on, then buff off with another clean towel. Photo courtesy Mother's.

A sawed-off paint brush has just the right amount of stiffness, yet is soft enough, to scrub this chrome-plated aluminum wheel without scratching it.

rather than brute force, to get the dirt and grime off. If you feel a polish is necessary, use the finest you can buy. Finish with a good wax.

Chrome-Plated Aluminum—Chromed aluminum wheels are found mostly on high-end cars: Beemers, Mercedes, some Corvettes and occasionally on Jaguars. These are usually dealer installed, aftermarket products. The dealer removes the wheels and has them sent out for chroming. Chroming over aluminum gives a higher gloss than chroming over steel—and they're a bit easier to maintain.

Machined Aluminum—In the same vein as above, treat machined aluminum wheels with a similar same deft touch. Machined wheels will appear to have been "turned" on a lathe. This leaves a series of very, very, fine grooves. Usually, this treatment will just be around the edge or a small band in the center. Treat this machining as carefully as you would burnished or anodized surfaces.

Unfortunately, you can't restore a machined surface as you did a burnished surface. If you tried the same steel wool technique, you'd end up with a burnished wheel rather than a machined wheel. Be careful.

Magnesium Wheels—Magnesium wheels were once so popular that the term "mag wheels" has become a generic term to describe any custom wheel, much like Kleenex™ is used to describe facial tissues. But wheels made from true magnesium are only found on classic cars, and are no longer made.

True magnesium wheels suffered from three significant drawbacks. First, the finish barely lasted a few months before it began to deteriorate, and they were easily pitted. Second, the early wheels had a tendency to crack and in some cases, break away from the hub. This problem was later rectified. The final big problem with the product was, magnesium is a flammable material!

The military uses magnesium flares

to light up the night on the battlefield. Powdered magnesium was the first material used in flash photography. Later, it was drawn into very fine wires and sealed in a glass bulb or tube, giving us what was called flashbulbs. In more than a few instances, when cars with magnesium wheels caught fire, so would the wheels, creating flames that firemen couldn't put out. Alloys were later added that ended this problem.

Restoring Mag Wheels—If you wish to restore a set of true mags, you're in for some real work. After cleaning them with a mag wheel cleaner, they must be sanded down to remove the layer of brownish oxidation that has been built up. Start with a 180 or 200 grit. Follow up with 320, 400 and 600. Beg, borrow or buy a small airtool that will accommodate a rotary buffing wheel. Using jeweler's rouge or a specially formulated magnesium wheel polish (Mother's and Eagle One both have one), buff out the fine scratches left by the 600-grit sandpaper to a lustrous sheen. The result will be the appearance of chrome, only softer and deeper. They are truly beautiful when fully polished. Be sure to follow up with a good wax.

People have tried for years to come up with a magic method to maintain the lustrous beauty of polished magnesium, with little or no success. They tried clearcoat paint, clear powder coating and all kinds of tricks—but nothing works as well as frequent maintenance, on a monthly or even weekly basis (depending on how much you drive). This is the only way to keep them looking good without having to restore them frequently.

At left is a full wire wheel with a knock-off hub. The rim is chromed steel and the spokes are stainless steel. A wheel spoke brush is almost a necessity to get them cleaned (you can get one from The Eastwood Co.). At right is an imitation steel wheel with a "wire basket." This is essentially a hubcap with spokes.

Wire Wheels and Wire Hubcaps

Next to restoring a set of magnesium wheels, cleaning real wire wheels used to be the most difficult task. It's still no small job but much easier with the two-step wire-wheel cleaning kits available today. These kits contain a spray bottle of chemical cleaner and a bottle of neutralizer. Spray on the cleaner, scrub, then spray on the neutralizer and hose off. The directions may tell you that scrubbing is not necessary, but in my experience, this is usually not the case. Unless your wheels are very, very clean, be prepared to scrub them.

For the scrubbing, a special brush has been designed just for wire wheels, available from the Eastwood Company. It allows you to get in and around the spokes with more ease than a regular flat scrub brush. With a bit of effort you can even get behind the spokes.

If you don't care to use the two-step wire wheel cleaner, there are other wheel cleaners available, but again, make sure you match the metal to the product. Check your wheels to see if they are all chrome or chrome rims with stainless steel spokes. Top-of-

the-line wheels will have the latter combination. Use a chrome cleaner where there is chrome and a stainless cleaner for the spokes. If you can't find a stainless cleaner, just use the chrome cleaner. These suggestions hold true for "wire basket" wheels as well.

TIRES

Tires are made with protective ingredients—"anti-oxidants"—that fight environmental attacks to the rubber. During hot, smoggy days, these ingredients come to the surface of the tire and look like a rusty, brown coating—a process called "blooming." A tire's worst enemy is ozone, an irradiated form of oxygen that breaks down the rubber bonds and causes superficial cracks to the sidewalls of the tire. Ozone is present everywhere, but often is worse in big cities, areas with poor air circulation and warmer climates. Along with road dirt, what you're seeing is accumulated brake dust. The old method for removal usually involved scrubbing for hours with a toothbrush.

Tire Products

Today, a variety of tire cleaners exist, but make sure that you get one with a neutral pH formula.

Aside from the pH factor, most tire products fall into three classes, the most popular being an all-purpose cleaner/polisher. Many of these products are "spray on, wipe off" or

There are many types of tire cleaners, and most work well. Some you just spray on and walk away from. You should get one with a neutral pH formula.

Many products say no wiping is necessary, but it really depends on how much grime and "blooming" the tire has. Scrubbing lightly with a medium bristle brush is called for in many cases.

just "spray on and walk away," types that will restore your tire in a simple step. Remarkably, these products actually do live up to their hype and do a credible job. If you use one of them, you'll be much further ahead if you do some scrubbing or buffing—even though the directions say otherwise.

As I said before, I favor a separate cleaner and dressing. I feel you get better results from products that only have one job to do, sort of like a specialist.

Some pros still use products such as Armorall Protectant to polish the tire after a good scrub-down with a strong detergent. Most of the companies who made these multi-use protectants have moved into the specialty product line with the Armorall company leading the way. It's hard to tell whether a tire has been polished with Armorall Protectant or Armorall FlashBlack, their new tire polish. Some of my detailer friends claim that the protectant gives too much shine. Their point being, that the idea of a tire

polish is to restore the tire to its original appearance—which was a soft shine rather than a glistening shine. It all comes down to what appeals to you.

Then there are the cleaners for white

sidewall tires. Westley's Bleche-Wite has probably been around the longest, and for good reason. It does a wonderful job on those classic sidewalls. But if you're having trouble finding it, try SOS™ or Brillo™ soap pads. These soap-saturated, steel wool pads are great for cleaning white sidewall tires. They work especially well where bad scuff marks have marred the tire surface, however they don't work as well when it comes to removing disc brake dust.

Cleaning Black Tires

The tire should already have been washed, assuming that you did so when you washed the entire car, or when you did the wheel. But before you attack the tire, scrub off any residual wheel cleaner and make sure it is completely dry. Now, spray the cleaner you've selected onto the tire. Apply it liberally around the outside surface. Don't attempt to clean the

Depending on the tire product directions, you may have to either rinse or wipe off the cleaner. Whatever method is used, make sure you get the tire as clean and as dry as possible before going on to the next step.

Few products rival Westley's Bleche-Wite for cleaning sidewalls. This '55 T-bird's whitewalls needed a serious touchup.

Westley's Bleche-Wite will not affect the black part of the tire, unlike some household cleaners, or bleach. Scrub around the entire perimeter, then rinse.

It is hard to tell that these whitewalls are over 10 years old.

tread area. This could result in a tire that fails to grip the road, causing a spin-out or failure to brake.

Allow the cleaner about five minutes to do its magic, then spray on another coat. This coat should be scrubbed. I suggest a brass bristle brush. Using extreme care, clean carefully in the groove where the tire joins the wheel. This is an area that traps dirt and must be deep cleaned. Be careful with the brush, especially around a painted wheel. You don't want to scratch it. Now rinse the tire. While you rinse, continue to scrub with your brush. The cleaner will be working deeply into the tire. To float out this dirt and cleaner you must continue to scrub while the rinse water runs. Dry the tire off with a clean towel.

If the towel has a great deal of black residue on it, repeat the process. More than likely it will be as black as the tire. You've dislodged a great deal of

dirt, brake dust and dead rubber—now get it all off. It might not seem like it, but you're only getting rid of a few mils of dead rubber that would fall off anyway. By the second scrubbing, the tire should be clean. Wipe it down well with a cloth towel, getting into that groove where the rubber meets the wheel. You should have a really clean tire now. (Be sure to chamois off the wheel at this time to prevent water spots.)

Cleaning White Sidewalls

There are three types of white accents on tires being manufactured today: the wide whitewall, the narrow whitewall and the white letters. Fortunately, all can be treated the same. If you elect to use the SOS pad, or as some do, steel wool and household cleaner, a word of caution is in order. Try not to get either of

these cleaners on the black part of the tire. They contain bleach which might result in a slight color change to the black. This can change the color to a brown/black shade that, on close inspection, is not the original look of the tire. The other products designed for whitewalls will not affect the black.

When doing whitewalls (wide, narrow, or letters), I use both a black tire cleaning product and a whitewall product. This may be a bit of overkill but again, we're going for the very best job possible. Clean the black part of the tire as described above, then do the white area. Spray on the cleaner, wait a few minutes for it to act, spray on another coat and begin scrubbing. Now you'll be getting off white oxidation rather than black.

After a thorough scrubbing, rinse. Again, continue scrubbing while you rinse. Pay particular attention to the black area of the tire. The loosened

If you have already polished the wheels, you will want to avoid getting any tire dressing overspray. Photo courtesy Mother's.

After wiping on the tire dressing, conditioner or protectant, use a clean, separate cloth to buff it well.

scrub, then rinse and scrub. Here, it will be very noticeable if the white oxidation clings to the black rubber. When your tire is as clean as it will be, it's time for polishing.

Polishing Tires

Dress tires using tire polish or dressing. The polish you use is also a protectant. It nourishes the rubber and helps keep the ultraviolet rays of the sun at bay. It also works to seal the tire against the effects of acids, oils, and dirt from the road. So be generous with its use. Remove excess dressing to avoid "dressing sling" from the tire surface. Generously apply a coating of tire dressing using a properly labeled safety bottle to all tires. Allow product to sit for a few minutes and wipe off excess dressing as required. Too much excess dressing will sling off the tire surface and redeposit on the vehicle once the vehicle is driven. Use caution when applying dressing to lightly colored vehicles with ground effects moldings. Dressing sling from tires can permanently stain the moldings. To avoid this problem, make sure you wipe down the tires thoroughly.

Avoid ordinary silicone emulsion protectants that cover over your surface contamination with a shiny, synthetic coating. These cause tire discoloration and decay.

CAUTION: Never, ever apply protectant to the tread of a tire. Doing so could result in a loss of traction.

white oxidation likes to plant itself into the black part of the tire giving an unprofessional appearance. Spray some cleaner on a dark, color-fast cloth and wipe it around the whitewall. If any white shows up on the cloth, give the tire another cleaning. There's still some oxidation.

White letters are treated the same way. Soak, reapply the cleaner and

Pristine interiors like this do not happen by accident. This show car is continually maintained by its owner, and it shows. Although the exterior paint gets the most public attention, where do you spend most of your time? Photo by Michael Lutfy

Personally, I feel the cleaning and detailing of the car's interior is the most important part of the detailing process. Why? Because that's where I am most of the time. Sure, the exterior attracts attention; the engine compartment is a great show-off. But, I only see those parts on occasion. I see the interior of my car all the while I'm driving, so I pay a lot of attention to the details of my interior.

The interior of your car takes as much of a beating as the rest of the car. You and your passengers are constantly tracking in mud, dirt, road tar, grease, engine oil and coolant (from walking across parking lots) and in the colder climes, snow and road salt. And how many meals have you eaten in your car? Many people nowadays eat in their cars, which inevitably leads to spilled food and drinks (coffee is a favorite). These are the inevitable mishaps that occur in today's helter-skelter lifestyle.

There are other "assassins" as well. The vinyl, leather, plastic and other materials used to construct the interior of your car are constantly emitting solvent vapors, the same vapors responsible for that "new car smell." These vapors land on the windows, seats, door panels and all other parts of the car. They too must be removed.

Finally, cigarettes, cigar and pipe tobacco produce oils (tar) in the smoke that permeate every nook and cranny of the interior, seeping into the fabric and are very difficult to remove. So, our interior takes a real beating. The best way to extend its life is to detail it frequently.

VACUUMING

The first thing that needs to be done is to thoroughly vacuum the interior.

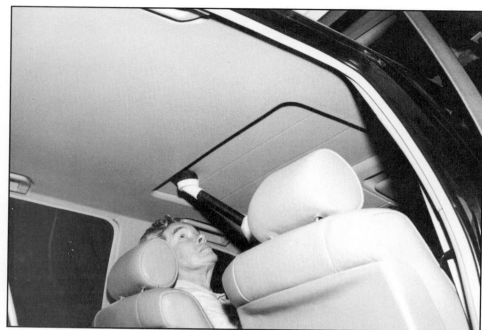

Begin vacuuming with the headliner and work downward.

The best tool for the headliner is the vacuum brush. Old headliners, or originals in classic cars, tend to deteriorate and weaken. The sharp-edged carpet tool could tear it easily. Use a soft bristle brush adapter if you have one available, otherwise, be very careful and move the vacuum back and forth slowly.

After a thorough vacuuming of the headliner, move to the instrument (dash) panel. Keep the brush tool on the hose. With a stiff brush, such as a cut-off paint brush, work the dirt out of the crevices of the instrument panel and then quickly grab it up with the vacuum. This helps prevent the loose material you brushed away from falling down into a lower crevice. When you finish the instrument panel, move to the door panels.

Vacuuming Leather—When vacuuming leather surfaces, use the brush tool as well. This prevents the possibility of scratching the leather. Vinyl and metal surfaces are not as delicate and you should use whatever

If you don't have a good shop vacuum, then you're better off going to a local car wash. You need a strong vacuum to do the job properly. The old Dustbuster is fine for minor pickups and maintenance, but at this stage, we need a lot of suction for deep cleaning.

Compressed Air

Use compressed air to blow dirt from cracks, under seats, between seats, AC vents and around windows front and rear. Use compressed air in conjunction with an OSHA-approved blow gun to blow dirt from cracks around front window, rear window, side panels, between seats, under seats, ac vents, center console, dash, etc. Be sure to wear eye protection during this procedure. Although it will be messy, you'll be picking it up next. This may seem like overkill, but we are detailing, not merely cleaning.

Vacuum Technique

Vacuum all interior parts, beginning with the headliner and moving downward. Make sure you get the ash trays, floor mats, carpets, seats, under seats, glovebox (remove personal items first) and door panels. Concentrate on thoroughly vacuuming the carpet and upholstery to remove as much dirt as possible prior to shampooing.

The brush tool helps to dislodge dirt in nooks and crannies, and won't scratch wood dashes.

FLOOR CLEANING

Where you begin deep cleaning is not so critical, but if the carpets need to be deep cleaned and shampooed, I recommend that you work this area first.

Vinyl Mats & Pads

Newer vehicles may have a vinyl pad underneath the pedals. For cleaning vinyl floor mats, I recommend Fantastik™. Other excellent products are 409 and Simple Green, and of course there are vinyl cleaners available from Eagle One and Meguiar's, as well as several other popular brands. Make sure you don't get any of these products on leather. They'll remove essential oils from leather, causing it to deteriorate faster than normal.

Begin with a diluted solution of the Fantastik or whatever cleaner you use, about 3/4-cup to 1-gallon of water. Other products should be used according to the manufacturer's directions. Spread this solution over the vinyl floor pad, let it soak for

Use a whisk broom to dislodge dirt from the floor before vacuuming. It will be more effective.

tool does the best job. If the door panels are cloth, you might want to switch to the broad carpet tool. This is good for really sucking up the dirt. Be careful, however, that it doesn't hook the fabric and tear it.

Seats—The seats must have special attention. Use the crevice tool where possible. Get around the seat belt retainers. If the seat back tilts forward, tilt it and get the grime that lurks between back and cushion. Use the whisk broom to get the areas between the seat cushion and the adjustment controls. If the headrest is sitting on the back cushion, lift it up and get the dirt hiding there. On all seats, make sure you vacuum the seams. Dirt lurks in there and will eventually cause wear and deterioration.

Floor—The floor of the car is always the dirtiest part. We track in everything listed above, and some of us, even more. Give the floor a good brushing followed by a very thorough vacuuming. Use both the carpet tool

and the crevice tool to get everything out. It may even be necessary to remove the trim-molding from the rocker-panel to get all of the soil collected in this area. In some cases, you may even want to remove the seats.

The floor of this truck is all vinyl. The most economical and effective method to clean it is to scrub it in a diluted solution of a household cleaner, such as Fantastik.

This simple shampooing machine from Sears will clean and almost dry any fabric, carpets, seats, etc. A fine stream of cleaning solution or clear water is emitted from a nozzle below the handle. The solution is immediately sucked up by the vacuum.

Before shampooing, spot stubborn stains with Resolve or 3M's General Purpose Adhesive Remover.

about five minutes, then go after it with a scrub brush. When you've finished scrubbing, wipe up the dirty solution with a wet towel, then repeat.

Stubborn, deep-seated vinyl stains may be removed with Westley's Bleche-Wite, the same chemical used to clean white sidewalls, but again, be careful not to get it on leather or the carpet.

Normally, after cleaning vinyl, you would follow up with a protectant. This is not the case with vinyl floor-covering. Protectant leaves a slippery film no matter how hard you buff. On a floor covering, the protectant can transfer to your shoes, and then to the brake pedal. The result could be your foot slipping from the brake at a most inopportune time, resulting in an accident. Save the protectant for the seats and door panels.

Shampooing Carpet

To do a really professional job, you'll need to shampoo the carpet with a commercial shampoo/vacuum unit. These are available for rent in many supermarkets, or at tool supply stores. Your local hardware store may be able to tell you where to rent one. There are industrial strength carpet shampoos that are available to go with

these units. P&S Sales offers a product called Enviro-Clean Extractor Shampoo Concentrate that works well with these combination shampoo-vacuums.

If you have not done so, remove the carpet pads and shampoo them first. As protectors, they get the most abuse and are frequently tracked with grease and oil from parking lots. These most likely will require greater effort to clean.

Pre-Spotting—Carpets and carpet mats should be pre-spotted with straight solution, or a supermarket product called Resolve™. For stubborn tar and grease stains, try 3-M's General Purpose Adhesive Remover. Apply a small amount to the spot, then use a towel to agitate to get the stain out. If you have to use a brush, make sure it is as soft as you can get away with so you don't damage the fibers in the carpet.

Test—Before you use any product, you should test it first to make sure it is compatible with the dye and material in your carpet. Find an

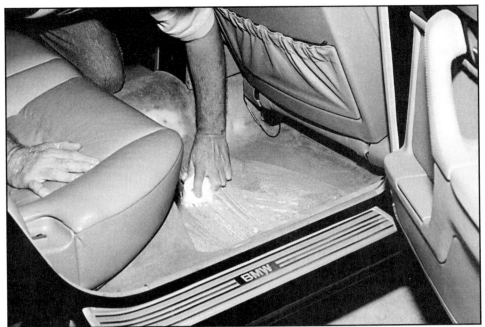

After applying shampoo, let it foam up and soak, then scrub. Avoid using a brush if possible; if not, use a soft bristled brush and apply light pressure to bring up dirt.

Floormats bear the brunt of abuse. Oil and tar stains will need to be scrubbed with adhesive remover.

Scrub the mat with shampoo, or if that doesn't work, a diluted solution of household cleaner. Afterward, rinse thoroughly, especially for deep pile carpet, then use a squeegee to get the excess water off. Allow to air dry completely in the sun.

inconspicuous spot, one not visible, and apply a small amount of cleaner. Wait a few minutes and check to see that the carpet hasn't faded.

Begin shampooing, with or without the power vacuum/shampoo machine, by starting with the carpet, then the upholstery and door panels if necessary.

If doing the project by hand, apply the product sparingly. Spray only enough foam or solution to wet the top of the fibers. Scrub with a towel, then dry with a clean towel. Most carpet shampoos do not need to be rinsed, and are vacuumed up. Concentrate on doing a thorough job. Visually you are sure to notice a difference but once you empty the recovery tank from the shampoo machine you will be amazed as to how much dirt has been removed. Make sure you extract thoroughly to remove as much water as possible to speed the drying process. If during the shampoo process some of the chemical shampoo solution has been sprayed up onto vinyl panels and trim go ahead and wipe them down with a damp cloth prior to moving on to the next procedure.

Scotchguard™—After the carpet is dry, spray with a dirt release agent such as ScotchGuard™. Although this product is advertised that it will prevent staining, in reality, it only

To keep a vinyl interior looking like this one, you'll need to wipe it down frequently with a protectant that has UV protection. Photo by Michael Lutfy

LEATHER INTERIORS

Nothing adds a finishing touch to a classic or modern automobile like beautiful leather upholstery. When properly cared for, leather upholstery will last far longer than other upholstery material and when premium hides are used will actually become more beautiful with age. Although there are leather cleaners and conditioners available from a number of manufacturers, few are as well versed in the subjects as the folks at Summit Industries, manufacturers of the leather cleaner and conditioner known as Lexol. Here's what Phil Meyers, Summit's vice president, has to say on detailing leather interiors:

"Cleaning and conditioning leather is very similar to caring for your own skin. Good skin care requires gentle cleaning and nourishment with moisturizers (oils) depending on your

allows the stain to be released easier. It's a good product, however, for this application.

VINYL INTERIORS

Many of our favorite cars and trucks of the '50s, '60s, and early '70s have vinyl interiors in them. While vinyl does not require as much maintenance as leather, a good care program will enhance its lifetime and its appearance. There are many vinyl cleaners and protectants. Some are all-in-one formulas, others are two-step. For deep cleaning, it is recommended that you wipe down all vinyl surfaces with a cleaner first, followed by a protectant/conditioner. For monthly maintenance, you may only need the all-in-one solution. Whichever protectant you use, make sure it is formulated to provide as much UV protection as possible. Some products for vinyl contain more silicone than other and produce a "slippery" finish. This may not be what you want for

the seats, and it definitely must not be applied to any vinyl mats or pedals. Let me repeat: Do not apply any protectant to vinyl mats! The protectant can transfer to your shoes.

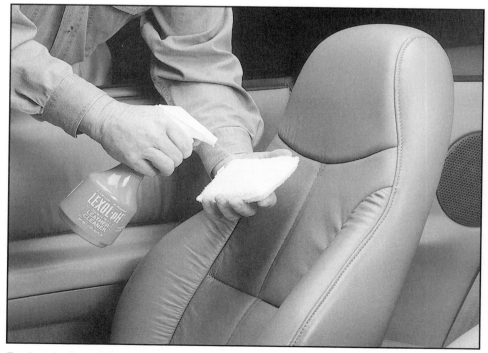

To clean leather, follow the same guidelines to care for your skin. The first step is to clean it, by applying a specially formulated leather cleaner, such as the Lexol brand above, to a sponge or clean towel. Photo courtesy Lexol

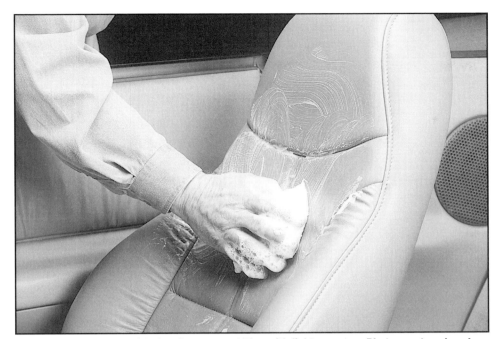

Work up a good lather with the cleaner, scrubbing with light pressure. Photo courtesy Lexol

skin type. Similarly, to safely clean leather you will need a neutral pH cleaner (between 4.5 and 7.5 pH) and a leather conditioner suitable for upholstery. To put this maintenance routine in perspective, keep this thought in mind. Cleaning and conditioning leather upholstery is very similar to bathing yourself out of a bucket on a camping trip. You need water to do the job, and you need to use the right amount of it. Soaking leather while cleaning it is not required any more than you would soak your face to wash it, and it can make drying time take much longer.

Prior to cleaning, vacuum your car's complete interior to remove any dirt and dust. The small dirt that accumulates in upholstery stitch lines works on threads to cut them and shorten their life. Using your leather cleaner, clean one section of the interior at a time, such as the seat back on one side, then the other and so on. Using lukewarm water, leave as much water in your cloth or sponge as if you were going to wash your face with

soap and water and apply your cleaner to one section of the interior with a gentle scrubbing motion. After washing this section, rinse your cloth or sponge to clear it of cleaner and

dirt, wring it out and wipe away the cleaner from the section you've cleaned, then towel dry it. Continue in this fashion, cleaning, rinsing and drying to finish the interior. An average car usually takes 15 to 20 minutes to clean.

Conditioning

As leather interiors take very small amounts of conditioner to properly care for them, premium, high quality products are your best choice.

Conditioning after cleaning is most effective as the cleaning process opens the leather's pores allowing the conditioner to penetrate deeper and quicker. Apply your leather conditioner to a slightly damp cloth or sponge and wipe in onto the leather. Dry, older and neglected leather can benefit by gently massaging the conditioner into the hide, and, multiple light coats of conditioner are

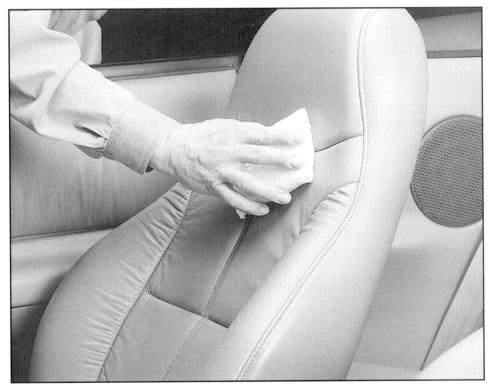

Rinse of cleaner with a damp sponge, as shown, then towel dry. Photo courtesy Lexol

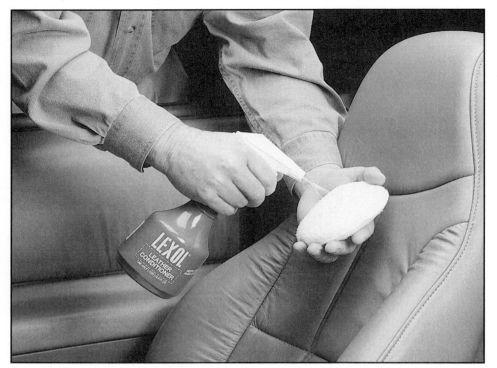

Traditional leather conditioners, like saddle soap, are not recommended for automotive leather. As with the cleaner, apply the conditioner to the sponge (do not use the same one you used to apply cleaner) rather than spray it on the seat or surface itself. Photo courtesy Lexol

project. Stains are almost impossible to remove. If the spot is something sticky like chewing gum or grease, the cleaner you use will probably remove it. Spray a generous amount of cleaner on the affected area and let it sit for a few minutes. With a very dull tool, such as a teaspoon, very gently scrape away whatever has been loosened with the application of cleaner. Several applications may be necessary to remove the material.

Be extremely careful with the scraping. Never use a knife or any sharp object. The surface of leather is both strong and fragile at the same time. It will wear forever but a sharp object will easily scratch it.

Saddle Soap and Neatsfoot Oil

Saddle soap is for saddles, not for

better when bringing back dry leather than soaking it in one massive application.

The entire leather interior of your car should be treated and then allowed 20 to 30 minutes to absorb the oils and preservatives. Then use a dry clean towel to vigorously rub down all of the leather surface and stitch lines to remove any excess conditioner.

Drying

After cleaning and conditioning a leather interior allow one to three hours to air dry, depending on outside temperatures and humidity. How often you will clean and condition your interior will depend on your car's use and its environment. Most often the look and feel of the leather will tell you when it's time to clean and condition again."

Spot Cleaning

Spot cleaning leather is a tricky

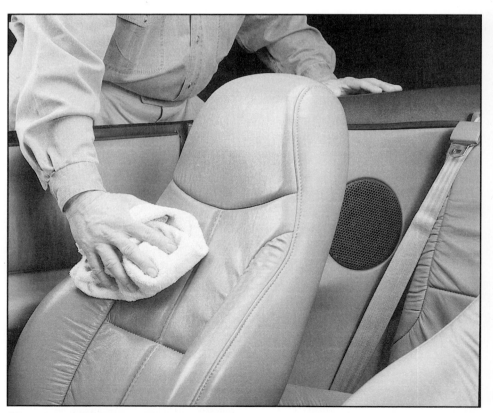

Allow the conditioner to soak, about 30 minutes, then buff off vigorously with a clean, dry cotton towel. Photo courtesy Lexol

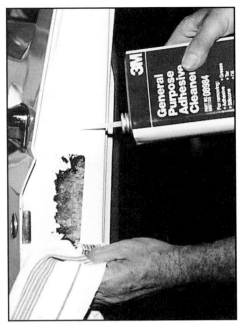

Get rid of unsightly door stickers with 3M's Adhesive Remover.

Door with painted surfaces may have scuff marks. A fine polish should work to buff them out.

leather seats. Neatsfoot oil is even worse. These two products, although great for most other leather products (baseball mitts, saddles, work boots), are inappropriate for leather used in upholstery and clothing.

Both saddle soap and neatsfoot oil may darken leather in great splotches. It soaks in quickly and its oil, though beneficial, darkens the leather. Save these products for other applications. If the leather you're cleaning is stiff and cracked, both of these products will make it more flexible but will stain (as above) and transfer to your clothing.

MISCELLANEOUS INTERIOR TIPS

Door Panels

Door panels are cleaned based on their material. For fabric, shampoo as described above. For vinyl, use a vinyl cleaner or Fantastik to wipe down the surface, then buff with conditioner. Likewise, use the appropriate cleaners/conditioners for leather.

On door panel armrests, you may encounter some stubborn stains, caused primarily from the oil on skin and hands that builds up on the armrest. Every time you get in the car, you grab the armrest to close the door. What's on your hand transfers to the armrest, and eventually the armrest gets pretty dirty. Sometimes the dirt and oil is so embedded, that simple household cleaners won't cut it.

One item that works well is 3-M's General Purpose Adhesive Remover, or any wax and silicone remover. If your panel incorporates cloth and carpet along with the vinyl, spray the solution onto a clean towel and use this to clean with. Keep all vinyl cleaners away from cloth or carpet.

Most dirt will wipe away when the cleaner is applied. Those spots that are tenacious will require some scrubbing. Use a small soft bristled brush to keep from transferring dirty cleaning solution to any areas that might be stained. When the panel is thoroughly cleaned, rinse it with a clean, damp towel.

Unfortunately, not only does the cleaner remove wax and silicone, it also can dry out the vinyl. All interior vinyl surfaces, with the exception of the steering wheel and floor mats (and possibly the seats) should be wiped down with a vinyl protectant after thoroughly cleaning the panel. Spray the protectant onto a clean towel, rub on, then buff off with a clean towel. I like to use a protectant that produces as little shine as possible.

Stickers—Today, most oil change reminders are made of vinyl and are attached to the top of the windshield on the driver's side (held there by static electricity). Only a few years ago, however, paper tags were glued to the door jamb with the reminder information. These are very difficult to remove with anything but our 3M adhesive remover. Squirt a little onto the old tag, let it soak for a couple of minutes, then scrape the paper off with your fingernail. Finish by washing the area with a clean towel soaked in cleaner. Clean the rest of the door with your cleaner of choice.

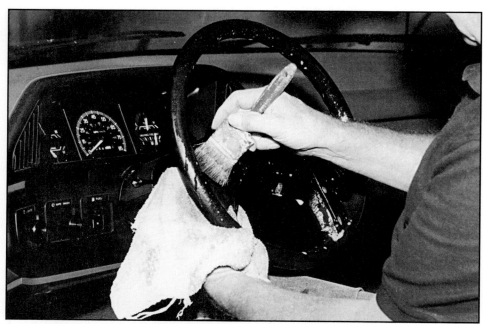

The steering wheel collects quite a bit of dirt and oils from hands. Fantastik or household cleaner will usually cut through it.

Scrub it good with a brush, wipe off the excess, and rinse with a clean, damp towel.

Scuff Marks—Our demonstration door had some scuff marks on the bottom of the door—probably from black-soled shoes kicking it. These were easily removed with a very non-aggressive buffing compound (Meguiar's Mirror Glaze).

Finish the door by cleaning and protecting the rubber weatherstrip. Apply some rubber and vinyl cleaner to a clean towel and clean the rubber. After cleaning the weatherstrip, protect it with a coat of protectant, applied as above.

Seats

Vinyl seats may need a little extra cleaning in and around the seams, and generally around the seat belt ports and anchors. As mentioned, when it comes to seats, make sure the protectant you choose does not contain a lot of silicone or other substance that makes it slippery.

If the seat you're working on has a welt (bead), pay special attention to what can collect in the groove between the welt and the top of the seat. Scrub this area out with a lot of vigor. Pull the seat-back forward and scrub the area between the back and cushion.

Bucket seats present no more problems than bench seats. A thorough scrubbing and rinse with a damp towel does the job. Be sure, as in the bench seat, to pull the seat-back forward and get things cleaned up down there.

Steering Wheel

You may have to use a lot of cleaner to get all the dirt off and some is sure to splash on the instrument panel. Unless the steering wheel is cleaned regularly, it can become excessively dirty. If there is excessive dirt, it will require a number of cleaning applications to remove this build-up. On vinyl and rubber, use Fantastik full strength. On leather-wrapped wheels, use leather cleaner. Be sure to get the backside, as this is often dirtier than the front. On vinyl or rubber, don't use a protectant. Again, the slippery effect of this product could cause you to lose your grip on the wheel.

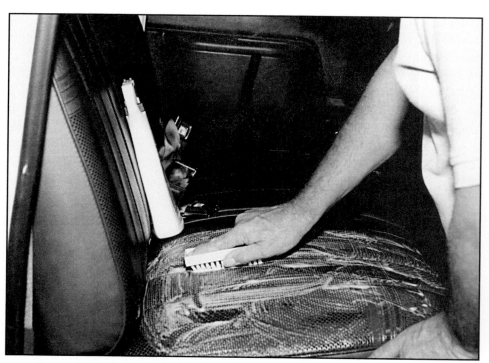

With vinyl or cloth seats, pay special attention to scrubbing the bead.

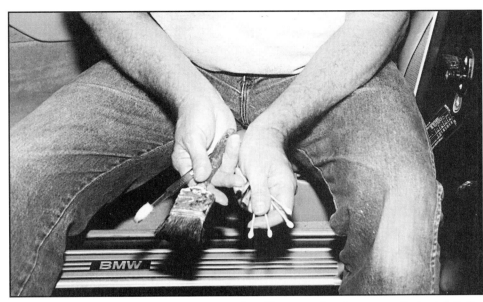

These tools are the stock in trade of a detailer. They are almost a necessity to detail the nooks and crannies of the instrument panel. From left to right: a toothbrush, cut-off paint brush, an acid swab and four cotton swabs.

The Instrument Panel

In the photo above, I'm holding my favorite instrument panel cleaning tools: a cut-off paint brush, tooth brush, acid swabs and Q-Tips. Here is the process I use to detail an instrument panel.

Earlier, you brushed and vacuumed, removing as much loose dirt as possible. Begin the process then with your cleaning solution. Most instrument panels are made of a number of different products requiring different cleaners. Many of these cleaners are not compatible with all the materials that make up the panel. Therefore, it's necessary to clean each surface independently. This means applying the cleaner to a specific area with a clean towel.

Our BMW instrument panel incorporates leather, plastic, vinyl, glass, stainless steel, and aluminum. We begin the process by cleaning the leather. Apply the cleaner to a towel and wipe down the leather. Be careful not to get this cleaner on any of the other parts. Finish by gently wiping with a damp-dry towel. It may be necessary to use a small, stiff brush such as a tooth brush or cut-off acid swab to get into the grooves. Dip the brush into the cleaner or carefully spray a little on the bristles prior to using it for cleaning.

When the leather is clean, turn to the plastic parts such as the fake-wood trim. Use Endust for this operation. The nice thing about this product is that it is one of the really effective products that cleans and polishes at the same time. Apply this product with a towel then buff with a clean one. Soft paper towels also work very well.

Clean the remaining plastic parts (radio face, control knobs, selector switches, and other small objects) with Q-Tips™ soaked in a very mild solution of Fantastik or similar cleaner. Dry with clean Q-Tips or other cotton-wrapped tool.

When the instrument panel is cleaned, apply protectant or conditioner to those areas requiring it. If you discover your instrument cluster lens is clear plastic or vinyl, use Meguiar's Clear Plastic Cleaner/Polish to remove any scratches.

Dip the Q-Tip in cleaner, then use a dry one to buff off any excess. It is tedious work, but this is what true detailing is all about.

Don't forget little details, such as the seatbelts, interior glass and ash trays, of course. Seat belts can be restored, or should be replaced if frayed. There are many OEM reproductions available from various classic car parts suppliers. This Corvette interior above is a frequent winner on the show car circuit. Photo by Michael Lutfy

and window cranks, armrests, knobs, and plastic trim. Don't try to dye a whole seat. It looks good for a few weeks but then begins to crack.

Seat Belts

Even the seat belts can be shampooed and made to look a whole lot better. Don't try to spot clean these products, it almost always leaves a stain. Instead, shampoo the entire belt. Use rug and seat shampoo. Resolve does not work too well for this operation.

Ash Trays

All ash trays used for cigarette ashes and butts should be removed from the car, emptied and then soaked for several hours in a strong soap and water solution. After soaking, scrub the tray until all signs of black tar have been removed. This not only improves appearance, it reduces odor.

Interior Glass

Prior to cleaning the windows remove any unnecessary window stickers or decals. Carefully use a razor blade scraper to scrape the stickers off of the window. If this is a retail detail keep in mind that the customer might prefer having them on his/her windows. Get customer approval prior to removing any. Use caution when working around the window defoggers. Scraping with a razor blade could damage the defogger heating elements.

Clean interior glass using a two-towel method for best results. This method employs one towel as the primary towel for the initial wipe after applying glass cleaner which removes the majority of the dirt and road film. The second towel is used for the final wipe down process to produce streak-free glass. The two-towel method consistently produces cleaner glass.

Dying Plastic Parts

Your local professional auto-paint supply has aerosol cans of vinyl dye that will match almost any interior. Sometimes, plastic and vinyl parts will fade or discolor from ultraviolet rays. These can be brought back by "painting" them with one of the vinyl dyes just mentioned. Clean the surface to be dyed with several applications of wax and silicone remover. Plastic parts are cast in a mold and much of the mold-release chemical remains on the part. This must be removed to make the dye adhere.

When the part has been cleaned with at least three good applications of cleaner, let it dry, then spray it with the aerosol dye just as you would any other paint job. Three light coats give a nice finished appearance with no runs. Heavy applications dry slowly and tend to run. Consider this for door

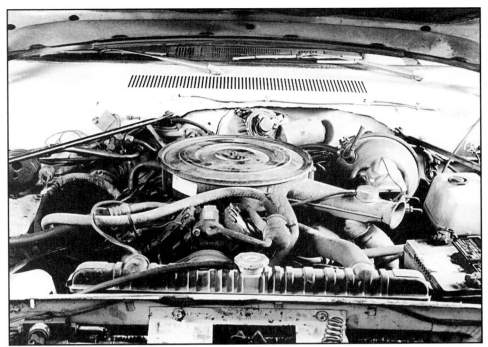

This is our project engine. Although it has never been cleaned before, it's tightly sealed, so there isn't a lot of oil all over the compartment. However, there's much to be done.

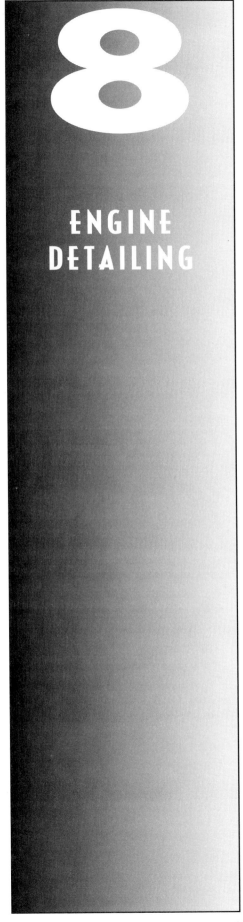

There's nothing more disappointing than to open the hood of an otherwise finely detailed vehicle only to find a greasy, oily mess. The engine compartment is no less important than any other area of the vehicle, and should be detailed as such. In this chapter, I illustrate as much detailing of the engine as is possible without removing it. Depending on the condition of your engine, you may or may not need to follow all of these steps. It depends on what your goals are, and how original you need to keep the engine.

Detailing the engine compartment can get as involved as removing various components for bead blasting and cleaning, repainting of parts, chroming and powder coating. You can limit yourself to just a good degreasing, or you can go all out and chrome the valve covers or paint accessory items (such as alternator brackets, for example). The choice is up to you, depending on how original you need to keep the car, and what

your budget will allow.

But the primary purpose is to remove the majority of the dirt and grease/oil from the engine and the compartment. To do so, you must use a degreaser, which may seem like a simple task, but it really isn't.

DEGREASING

Cleaning and degreasing the engine compartment may seem like a simple task but in fact it can be one of the most difficult in terms of potential damage and risk both to the vehicle and to the environment. It is very important that you take caution when applying aggressive cleaning agents that could potentially stain if used improperly.

Also you run the risk of causing potential harm to numerous electronic parts when using water under the hood in conjunction with strong degreasing agents. If done properly this process can be effectively completed without damaging the vehicle.

The environment of course is a

Use your degreaser of choice. Before you begin, make sure you wash surrounding painted surfaces, both inside and out, with car wash solution, leaving a heavy layer of suds as a barrier against the degreaser. I find that the penetrant WD-40 works particularly well. If I were using another, more caustic degreaser, I'd be wearing gloves. Make sure the engine is cool.

A strong stream of water will blast away the loosened grease and grime. Keep the run-off away from growing things and out of the sewer system.

If you have access to it, use compressed air to dry the engine.

concern with regards to both the chemical being used and the grease and dirt that has been removed and rinsed off the motor.

Products

There are many different degreasers to choose from. Perhaps the most popular is Gunk, which has been around for years. They have a product called Engine Brite that works well, but it is caustic. My friend and co-author for several HPBooks, Larry Hofer, recommends and uses WD-40.

Use the same precautions you would use with any other cleaning product.

Cautions—The heaviest degreasers

may be flammable, and can irritate your skin. The vapors may be harmful. Some degreasers are environmentally safe, but the stuff they wash off isn't. The grease and oil run-off from the motor can get you a pretty stiff fine in many neighborhoods. Make sure you check the local laws. The best advice is to degrease the motor at a manual car wash that has a regulated, designated area for degreasing engines. You can then use your own degreaser, and you have the added benefit of a high pressure hot water system.

If you really want to know the science behind degreasers, check out the sidebar on page 91.

Technique

Because the degreaser is generally caustic, you should wear safety glasses and chemical resistant gloves. Make sure the engine is completely cool, as well as the paint. You should

How Soaps & Detergents Work Together To Clean Grease

Courtesy P&S Sales

There has been a recent increase in interest in strong, low VOC degreasers. In general degreasing cleaners use three mechanisms for breaking down and removing grease and oil: 1) dissolving the grease with a solvent, 2) encapsulating the oils with detergents so that they can be washed away with water and 3) chemically changing the oils so that they can be washed away with water. Most degreasers use a combination of all three of these techniques.

Grease & Oil

Grease is merely a thickened version of oil. Strangely enough, the oils are usually thickened with specialized soaps, for instance lithium grease uses lithium based soaps, thus the name. Most of these soaps are not soluble in water so they don't aid in the cleaning process so, for simplicity, we'll consider grease and oils the same thing. Oils are medium length chains of carbon atoms, 12 to 20 carbon atoms long, that are insoluble in water. If an end of the oil is altered so that one end is water soluble you now have a detergent, or soap, depending on how it has been altered.

Caustic

Caustic soda is one active ingredient in the soap making process. Fats and oils from plants or animals are mixed with a caustic to turn them into soap. By mixing oils with caustic, an end of the molecule is altered so that it mixes with water, creating a soap molecule we talked about in the second paragraph. Almost any natural fat or oil will work in soap making. That is why you find soap made with olive oil, called castille soap, or soaps made with cocoa butter, which is oil from a coconut.

Caustic chemicals are chemicals with a high pH, over 11.5. They are very reactive chemicals and they will turn most oils into a soap.

It follows that, if you can turn the oil you're trying to clean into a soap, it will be a lot easier to clean. So, detergent manufacturers put in a little extra caustic in soap and detergents which help turn the oils to be cleaned into soap. This is a major reason why degreasers are so caustic. Since the user is going to be cleaning a lot of grease and oil, the formulator puts a lot of extra caustic into the cleaner to break down the grease and oil into soap.

Detergent

As mentioned earlier, detergents are molecules with one end that mixes with water and one end that mixes with oils. It sort of makes sense that if you have a mixture of oil, water and detergent then the various parts will orient themselves to mix together and an emulsion forms. The average detergent emulsion is a blend of oils and water where all the oil droplets are surrounded by detergent molecules. The water mixing sides stick out into the water, like a pin cushion with lots of pins.

Butyl

Butyl cellosolve is a version of a group of solvents, called glycol ethers, that have the fairly unique ability to mix with both oils and water. Butyl cellosolve can dissolve the oils to be cleaned and make it easier for the other ingredients to wash the oils away. So Butyl can easily be added to a water based cleaner, since it dissolves in water, and then start dissolving grease when it is needed. When the grease is pre-dissolved by the butyl, the detergent and caustic can more easily grab the dirt and oils and wash them away.

do this operation in the shade or a covered area. To prevent any staining from the chemical degreaser, rinse and wash down the surrounding areas near the engine compartment with water and car wash soap before you open the hood. This includes the fenders, grille and wheelwells. Make sure you apply a lot of suds, and do not rinse off. This will limit the risk of potential chemical staining or streaking.

When applying and rinsing chemicals with a pressure washer or water hose, limit the amount of contact with electronic areas contained within the motor compartment. If you have a

Use a flare-nut wrench when removing the nut retaining the fuel line to the carburetor. This will prevent rounding the shoulders of the nut.

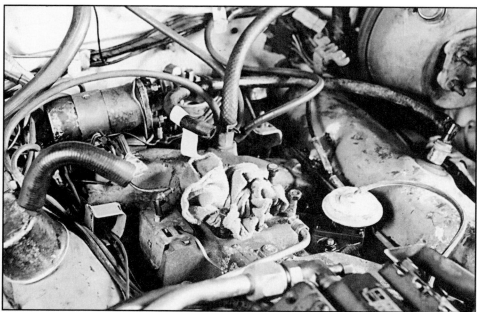

After removing the carburetor, stuff a towel into the manifold to keep foreign objects like nuts, bolts, and tools from falling in. That piece could find its way into a cylinder and destroy the engine.

carburetor, remove the air cleaner and stuff a rag into the venturis. You should cover your distributor, electronic components, carburetor, intake system and all underhood wiring and sensors.

As with the surrounding body parts, rinse and apply car wash suds to the painted surfaces surrounding the engine to help prevent chemical staining.

Now you should use a water hose or pressure washer to wet down the entire engine once again. The purpose of this step is so that the cleaning solution used will spread out more evenly, thus reducing the amount of chemical required to clean the motor compartment.

Apply the degreaser and follow the directions for the length of time you need to let it sit to work effectively. As you apply the degreaser, try to keep overspray off of any painted areas. If you have areas of excessive grease in any one area, you may need to scrub it well with a parts brush.

Make sure that you do not allow the loosened grease, dirt and degreaser to dry out. This will cause the grease to re-adhere to the surface, and you're back where you started. After the appropriate amount of time, rinse the entire compartment with a high pressure water hose.

If you don't have access to one, you can buy a brass tip for your garden hose that reduces the size of the hose opening down to about 3/8-inch. If you've got 40 pounds of water pressure or better, you can blast everything away, including some of your paint after the degreaser has soaked in.

PARTS REMOVAL

Now that the engine is degreased and dry, you can inspect it more closely to assess the level of detailing necessary. Depending on the condition of your engine, you may or may not find it necessary to remove some of the components and

recondition them. I'm not suggesting a full on restoration, but a little spray paint in certain areas can go a long way. Some parts can be sandblasted, or thoroughly cleaned in a parts dip that is much more effective than the engine degreaser. In the photos, I removed the battery and battery tray, air cleaner, carburetor, distributor cap, coil, some of the hoses, the two valve covers, and other minor parts and pieces in a restored Plymouth Valiant.

To help with disassembly, I recommend that you buy one of the HPBooks engine rebuild books that corresponds to your car or get a factory shop manual, or a Chilton or Haynes guide for your car or truck. Every detail of disassembly you'll be doing is fully described and demonstrated therein. It could save you hours of headaches should you forget what goes where.

Because you'll be taking things apart, even the best of us can quickly forget how something goes back together. Therefore, I recommend that

Here's our valve covers next to the ignition wires. They look pretty humble now. In an hour they'll look brand new.

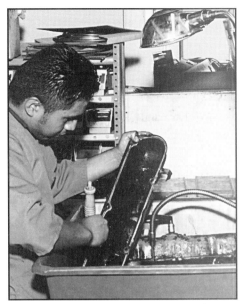

Art Gonzales, one of the talented craftsmen at Design Engineering, demonstrates the type of cleaning required of restoration projects. He begins by cleaning our valve covers in a solvent tank.

you put masking tape tags on everything, with notes as to where it goes. It's much easier to tag each spark plug wire than to get out the manual, find the firing order, try to figure out which wire is number one, and then wind-up getting one of the wires on the wrong plug anyway. You'll thank me over and over when it comes time to put it all back.

Another big help is a Polaroid camera to record the item as it sits on the car. If the component's removal is complicated you may want to take this step.

Battery

Always remove the battery first. This prevents the possibility of shorting something out and causing a spark. Sparks lead to fires. Removing the battery can also prevent damage to tools and to the tool user.

I strongly recommend removing the battery clamp and the battery tray. These should be cleaned as described below and repainted outside the car. Acid from the battery rusts and corrodes the parts. To prevent further

decay, these parts must be thoroughly reconditioned.

Valve Covers

Valve covers are either chromed or painted. If the paint is chipped, you should have them blasted or stripped and repainted. When they're out of the car, remove any smog attachments if you can get them off without bending or breaking anything. In our photos you'll notice we were unable to pull the PCV from the valve cover. The only problem this presents comes when it's time to paint. That problem was easily overcome with a little masking tape.

Air Cleaner & Carburetors

If your car has a carburetor, the air cleaner and carb can be removed to be cleaned up thoroughly. These items dominate the engine compartment, so it is important to get them reconditioned and detailed. Tag each carb part for its location, make a drawing, or take pictures so you can get it back together. Remove all the

rubber vacuum hoses and mark them too.

To remove the fuel line, you'll need a fuel-line wrench.

Finally, remove the nuts and bolts retaining the carburetor to the intake manifold.

Usually there are two bolts and two studs (in the manifold) captured by two nuts. If the studs come out, be sure to put them back in the right place, after removing the nuts.

Be sure the gasket stays on the manifold as you remove the carb. Many gaskets will fit several ways. There are openings for fuel and air that must align with the fuel and air ports. Therefore, carefully examine the way the gasket sits on the manifold and mark it accordingly. This way, when you replace it, all the ports will line up and the fuel and air will flow properly. When you remove the gasket, be sure to stuff a rag or towel into the intake port(s) to keep foreign objects from falling into the manifold.

After drying them, he places them in the bead blaster and removes all the paint and rust. Bead blasting is a less abrasive method for removing paint and rust.

Ignition Wires and Distributor Cap

Mark the ignition wires for their correct location, even if you're going to replace them. I number them with masking tape from front-to-rear with a "P" or "D" denoting passenger or driver's side. Leave the wires intact in the distributor cap and remove the cap from the distributor. Remove the rotor and tape or wire it to the distributor cap. If you leave it on the distributor, you'll knock it off.

If you leave the plugs in the block, wrap some masking tape around them. Paint on the plugs is really amateurish.

RECONDITIONING

Reconditioning begins with a good cleaning of the engine components. The best method is to thoroughly immerse them in a parts cleaning solvent.

The best way to clean your parts

will be to gather them all up, take them to your local machine shop or garage, and ask them to clean them in their cleaning (solvent) tank. These are sometimes called "hot tanks." The solvents used by professionals are stronger (and work faster) than anything you can buy off the shelf from your local parts house.

If you haven't access to the above, or simply want to do it yourself, there are a number of cleaning solvents available to you at your local auto parts house or paint store. If you buy one of these many solvents, don't buy lacquer thinner. Lacquer thinner is too volatile, is very hard on your lungs and skin, and evaporates too fast to really do a good job. Of the paint solvents, mineral spirits work best. Never, ever use gasoline or kerosene as a solvent ! The risk of fire far outweighs any beneficial aspects of gasoline as a solvent.

Bead Blasting

The next step is to remove any paint

and rust. Remember, we're trying to detail the engine for show condition.

Bead blasting is a wonderful method for stripping paint and rust, particularly manifolds. Again, a machine shop should have bead blasting service available, as will a company that does powder coating, which is a high temperature process whereby the coating is literally baked into the metal.

Bead blasting is a more gentle, less abusive form of sand blasting. Rather than using sand as the abrasive medium, microscopic glass beads are used. Where sand, under pressure, and traveling at a high rate of speed, will eat right through metal, glass beads under lower pressure will not affect the metal. It will, however, rapidly eat up rust and paint leaving only clean, bare metal.

Paint Stripper & Rust Remover—If bead blasting is simply not practical, you can use a paint stripper and rust remover.

The valve cover now looks just as good as new. Note the masking tape around the PCV valve.

This is the top of the air cleaner undergoing the three-step process of painting. A tack coat, then a color coat, and finally, a gloss coat.

I think you'll agree that this piece looks just as good as a baked or catalyzed enamel.

The battery tray receives three coats of black paint. Most of the ancillary parts of the engine compartment are painted black. Usually, it's just the engine block, manifold, oil pan, and valve covers that are painted a color. Our Plymouth parts are painted Chrysler blue.

Painting Parts

I like to paint as many of the parts, brackets and accessories as possible. There are high temperature paints specifically formulated for this task, available from the Eastwood Company and auto parts stores. Make sure you mask off all areas that you want to keep clean. Buy one roll of 1-inch masking tape and one roll of masking paper, 24-inches wide. Regular newspaper is okay as a substitute as long as you use twice as much, because it is more porous.

Technique—Painting small areas with aerosol cans can be just as effective as painting with a professional system if you follow a few simple guidelines, the most important of which is: two thin coats are more effective than one heavy coat.

Paint in aerosol cans is about 90 percent carrier and 10 percent pigment. To get full coverage with so little "color" (pigment) requires laying on a lot of material. If you try to lay it all on at "one shot," it's so thin it runs

right off. The result, of course, are runs or sags. These are easily avoided by taking your time and applying two or three coats.

First, although your part looks stunningly clean, and is probably down to bare metal, wipe it down, using a clean towel, soaked in wax and silicone remover. This will get off the last bit of oil, grease, or silicone

Masking an area is quite easy. I've just tossed two pieces of masking paper on each side of the radiator and held them in place with two or three strips of tape.

that may be remaining. Clean twice and paint once.

Your part may or may not need a primer. If it does, follow this three-step process, then apply the color paint using the same three-step process.

Spray one light coat, called the "tack coat," over the entire area to be painted. For us it will be a whole valve cover or the entire top of the intake manifold. Lay down only enough paint to show there is some color over the full surface.

The second coat is called the "color coat." With fast drying paint, such as used in aerosol cans, the tack coat is immediately dry. Follow up with a second coat that only gives full color to the part. There should be no "holidays" where bare metal or old color is showing through. This coat will take a little longer to dry. If you're painting all the parts one color, by the time you've finished the last part, the first part will be dry enough for the third coat.

This coat is called the "gloss coat." There's now enough paint on the part to support a third and heavier coat. Spray the third coat a little heavier

than the second. Just enough to make the paint flow without running. This will give you a nice, run-free coat with lots of gloss.

After painting the valve covers, air cleaner, battery tray, and other removed pieces, I turned my attention to the parts still in the engine compartment. Here, you'll need to do a little masking and some taping.

Masking Techniques—For the type of painting we're doing in this engine compartment, we don't have to be too

fancy. We just want to keep paint from one part getting on other parts. If something must have a closely defined edge, make that edge first with masking tape, then use masking paper.

Not all areas of masking paper need be fully taped, either. Note the photo at left where I'm painting the top of the radiator. I just stuck two sheets of masking paper over the front of the car and behind the radiator, holding each in place with two or three pieces of tape. Nothing fancy—just enough to keep paint off of everything but the radiator, and not let the wind blow the paper away.

As with all of the job, you can make the masking and painting as thorough or as "quick" as you want it to be. You could unbolt the air conditioner and move it out of the way, or paint it in place (as I did). You could take the fan off and paint it, then get behind the radiator or just paint the blades of the fan. The depth of the job is up to you.

Polishing

On many of today's cars with

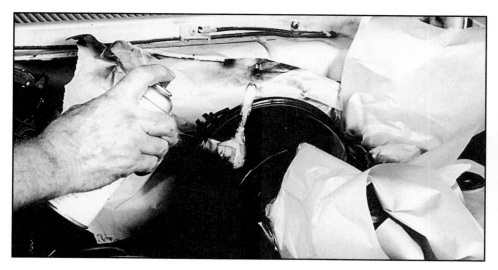

Although this brake booster was not painted black originally, we're looking for cleanliness, not originality. Notice, however, I'm not painting the master cylinder. Master cylinders are never painted because brake fluid, which always leaks out, will eat right through the paint. Just leave the master cylinder as is.

Here's the intake manifold looking good. Note the paper in the ports to keep things from falling in. Notice also I have returned the nuts and bolts to their original location. This keeps me from losing them or replacing them with the wrong size.

I want to paint the exhaust manifolds black. To do so requires a special paint called high heat paint. It will hold up to temperatures under 1200 degrees. Don't use your regular engine paint for the exhaust.

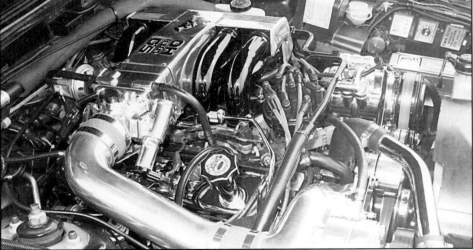

The middle and bottom photos illustrate the difference between chrome plating and polishing. The middle Corvette engine has just about every nut and bolt chromed. Some would say that's over-doing it. The bottom photo has most of the main engine parts polished, which gives a more natural appearance. Photos by Michael Lutfy

aluminum parts, sending those parts to a professional polisher will add luster to your car making most people think you've had extensive chroming done. Unlike chroming, however, polished metal is hard to keep up. It must continually be maintained with hand polishing, but is sure looks good.

Chrome Plating

Chrome plating is another popular choice and if done by the right shop, can be very resistant to the elements. Really fine chrome plating, what is called in the trade as "triple plating," is very expensive.

Powder Coating Or Powder Painting

As noted briefly, there are companies that will coat your parts with a porcelain type of finish called powder coating. You can get this coating in a very wide variety of colors—many of which are formulated to match your car's color scheme. I prefer powder coating to painting for its durability. There is still

Where brushing is not necessary, wipe all the surfaces with solvent. Again, wipe up the excess and use a two application process.

To make this edge look better, I'm scraping away the old paper tags glued to this area. The printing can no longer be distinguished and they look really ugly.

some question, however, about its use in show cars.

Some judges still mark you down because it was not "an original" finish. It has been agreed by all, however, that powder coating the frame of a car, no matter how old, will not be grounds for point deductions. So, if you're into showing in original class, ask around the car clubs how the judges feel about powder coating.

Other Platings

There are several other plating options available to you. Among these

are zinc chromate, cadmium, nickel, brass and copper.

Cadmium, or just cad plating, has been very popular throughout the years, especially the fifties through the seventies. Many nuts, bolts, lines and fittings were cad-plated.

Other Options

There are a number of companies that actually sell complete engine dress up kits for popular engines, such as the Chevy small-block. These kits usually include matching valve covers, pulleys, brackets and air cleaners that are anodized, polished,

chromed or plated in the same manner. Moroso and B&M are two examples that offer these items.

Final Details

The last of the parts to be detailed are the hoses and electrical wires. All of the hoses must be washed with wax and silicone remover or one of the other solvents you may have purchased. Again, beware of lacquer thinner. It will damage hoses and electrical lines. When the hoses are clean, shine them up a bit with a rubber or vinyl reconditioner.

ENGINE COMPARTMENT

Although the engine is degreased, the inside of the engine compartment needs to be cleaned by hand. There's no quick way to do this. Get a bunch or rags, towels, scrub brushes and your gallon can of wax and silicone remover. Start at the top and work down. I clean the firewall first, then the fender wells.

Wash an area then wipe off the soiled residue. Wash the area again and wipe it once more. Usually, two washes and wipes will get the surface clean enough to paint. These washes may need to be done with scrub brushes. Do it as described above: wash and wipe twice.

When the metal parts are done, turn your attention to the hoses and wiring. These are best done with a towel or rag saturated in cleaner, then wiped down with another clean towel. Depending on how dirty things are, usually, one wash and wipe is enough.

You must be the judge of how far you want to take the cleaning part of the job. I went only far enough to get most of the grease and grime off the surface you could see. With further

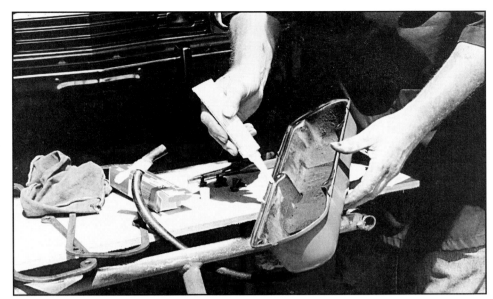

The gaskets should be cemented into the valve cover. However, the gasket should not be cemented to the heads. If you do cement them to the head and cover, you'll probably damage the cover the next time you have to remove it.

With not too much difficulty, I was able to get the carburetor and its linkage back on to the manifold. I still have a towel in the throat of the carburetor to keep extraneous parts out of the venturis. When you mount the carburetor, don't forget to remove the paper you had in the manifold.

effort I could have removed more parts and cleaned deeper and deeper. At some point, however, it makes more sense to take the whole engine out and start from scratch, which is something you can plan for when you are ready for your next engine rebuild.

Polishing & Waxing—Because areas are painted surfaces, they can be treated with the procedures outlined in Chapter 4. Use touch-up paint for paint chips and scratches, and use cleaners and polishes to remove scratches and small defects. The surfaces can then be coated with a good carnauba wax.

ASSEMBLY

Valve Covers

Valve-cover gaskets are not very expensive and should be replaced any time you remove the cover. Heat and oil make the old gasket hard and brittle and usually cracked. You can never get the gasket back on the head in the exact location from which it was removed. The results: oil leaks. So, buy a new set of gaskets and

watch while I replace those from the Plymouth.

The old gasket will have been removed during the cleaning process. You must, however, make sure that all bits and pieces of the old gasket have been removed. Cleaning does not always get the little bits and pieces that may be burned into the metal. When the gasket surface is surgically clean, straighten any bent edges with a pair of pliers. These are usually very minimal bends, dings and nicks. Major problems must be taken care of before painting.

When you're ready to place the gasket onto the cover, run a narrow bead of silicone around the inside of the cover where the gasket will lie. Run the bead around the circumference of each bolt hole. Drop the gasket in place, check to see that the bolt holes are correctly aligned and there is no cement clogging them. Now let the cement dry for 30 minutes while you do something else.

Carburetor

I worry most about getting the

carburetor and the ignition wires back on (correctly) so I go right to work on the carb as the next piece to install. Carefully check all around the intake manifold to be sure there are no little parts, nuts, bolts, or tools that could fall in, then carefully remove the towels you have in the intake port. Replace the gasket, in the correct orientation to avoid the above described problems of fuel and air flow. Then gently place the carburetor over the two studs. If it fails to seat, do not force it. Determine why it's not seating, correct the problem. Then reseat it.

To get the nuts onto the studs may require that you lift the carburetor up a little. Often, there's not enough room between the top of the stud and the body of the carb to get the nut in. Don't run the nut down yet. Now install the two bolts.

Every manufacturer does things differently. Some carburetors must have the two bolts passed through the

Wrap the electrical wires with electricians tape to refresh their appearance.

Clean ignition wires set off the engine. Don't forget to lace the wires through the clips.

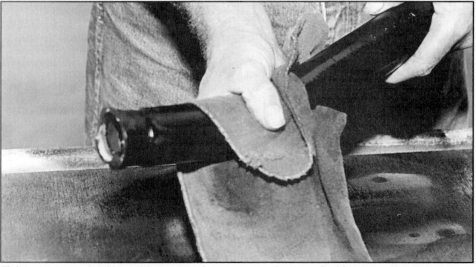
Finish the hose detailing with a coat of protectant. Don't omit this step. Not only does it make the hoses look nice, it helps prevent cracking.

body before you try to seat it over the studs. Some carbs will have to be lifted, as before, to get the bolts in. Some older cars have no bolts, only studs—or vice versa. The point is, it's going to take a little exercise and patience to get it in and seated.

When it's down with all fasteners in place, run the nuts and bolts down finger tight. Next, tighten each nut and bolt, in a clockwise manner, about 1/4-turn at a time. The base of the carburetor is quite brittle and easily cracked. Therefore, the pressure on each corner must be about the same throughout the tightening process. If you have a shop manual, find the torque settings for the nuts and bolts and tighten them accordingly.

Without a torque wrench and torque measurements, tighten the nuts and bolts until they're very snug then stop. When everything is back together, start the engine and watch for gas leaks around the base of the carburetor. If there are none, the bolts are tight enough. If there are leaks, tighten the bolts only enough to stop them.

Get out your pictures, drawings or shop manual to help you get the throttle linkage and vacuum lines all back in place. If you failed to take my earlier advice, you may have to call in a mechanic friend at this point to get all of this laced back together. I was fortunate. I consulted all of the above and got it together right the first time. That has not always been the case.

Distributor Cap and Ignition Wires

The next big worry is the electrical system. I know you'll have marked everything and will have no problems but let me remind you of a few things. First: don't forget the rotor. Put it back on before you replace the distributor cap. Second: with a little effort, you can force the distributor cap to go on 180-degrees off. Of course, there's no way the engine will run this way. Be sure the notch in the distributor cap aligns with the stud on the side of the distributor, assuring yourself (and the engine) that the distributor cap is correctly located.

Your third concern is that the ignition wires do, in fact, make good, full contact with the spark plugs. Most ignition wires have a boot at the business end of the wire to seal out moisture, grease, and oil. It's very easy to slide the boot over the plug and not have the wire make contact with the metal tip of the plug. If possible, pull the boot up until you can see the clip at the end of the wire. Assure yourself that this clip is firmly attached to the plug, then slide the boot down over wire and plug. Finally, route the wires through the clips on the valve covers so that everything looks neat.

Final Details

For our Plymouth, the last things to do were to replace the battery tray, the oil and tranny dipsticks, the air-cleaner and PVC parts, and finally, the battery. Again, this can be a place for problems.

Be absolutely certain that the positive cable goes to the post with a (+) sign next to it and the ground cable goes to the post with the (-) mark next to it. The positive cable is almost always red in color unless some ding-a-ling has changed it. If both are black or some other color, follow each to its mounting point. The positive cable will originate from the

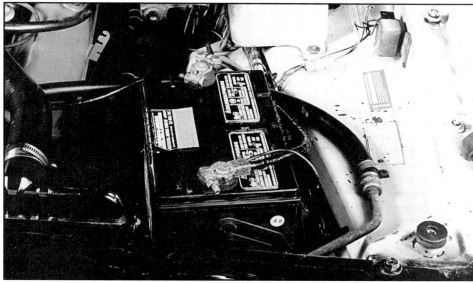

If there's a lot of corrosion on the battery, use baking soda and water to clean it off. Oil and grease may be removed with solvent. Finish the detailing of the battery with vinyl and rubber conditioner.

As you can see from the original photo, this engine has been completely transformed.

starter or starter solenoid, and the negative, or ground cable will be bolted to the frame (or possibly to the engine). If your car is pre-1955, all bets are off. Some of the old six-volt cars had positive grounds, rather than negative. If the car you're working on was built before 1960, check the owner's manual and ignore my directions.

9

CAR COVERS

Text & Photos
by John Pfanstiehl

It is possible to get tailored car covers at a reasonable price for the more popular cars. Note the pouches for the mirrors.

After all of your hard work, it only makes sense to make every effort to keep your vehicle as clean as possible. Of course, keeping your car garaged is the best and most obvious step you can take, but even then, you should consider a car cover.

There are almost as many kinds of car covers as there are kinds of cars. A little research and planning can make the difference in whether the cover helps or hurts you.

CHOOSING A COVER

The first question to ask yourself is the intended use for the cover. Car covers are desirable even for collector cars that are garaged most of the time. A cover will keep the dust off the paint and chrome so that the car looks its best any time you wish to show it. Also, the car has to be cleaned less often, which is not only a major savings in time and effort, it is often to the car's benefit. Show chrome and flawless black or dark colored paint jobs can get scratched incredibly easy.

In many cases, the less they have to be cleaned the better.

A third benefit of covering stored cars is the protection against bumps and scrapes. Whether the potential damage is from children and other traffic in your garage or from work going on in a commercial building, having a layer of soft material on the side of your car can prevent disfiguring scrapes, scratches, or gouges. Therefore, if inside storage is the main use of the cover, having a thick material (such as a heavy fabric with a soft liner) may be your best choice. However, such a heavy cover may be too bulky for use on a car which is driven often. It is more difficult to put a thick cover on, and it takes up a lot of space in the trunk!

If the cover will be frequently used outside, it is important that it fits snugly. Elastics or draw strings are needed so that the cover can be tied down to prevent it from flapping excessively in the wind. Too much movement can allow the paint to be abraded or allow the cover to tear.

Outdoor use also requires a cover

Custom made-to-fit car covers can be obtained for a price for just about any shape car. This thick felt-lined cover from Beverly Hills Motoring Accessories was made to fit the body contours of a 1959 Cadillac, and it cost under $200.

material that will breathe. It is inevitable that the cover will get rained on at some time and, if the moisture can't escape, the cover can do more harm than good.

A car cover can also be an enhancement to an expensive car. In that case, having the cover custom-made and fitted to the body style is an important consideration. Some car marques are popular enough so that a fitted cover is available off-the-shelf. Corvettes, Porsches, Mercedes, Camaros, and Mustangs are prime examples. Other marques are sufficiently in demand that manufacturers who specialize in making car covers already have a pattern for them. If you order a cover, they will cut it out and sew it up for you at a reasonable price.

Before ordering the cover, decide if any special features are needed. Examples of special features are pockets sewn in for the mirrors, a hole or boot for the antenna, a zippered flap on the side for easy entrance to the driver's side door (particularly useful when the car is transported in certain types of enclosed trailers), or grommets for tie-downs or a security lock.

This cover looks securely fastened and it is. The problem is that wind caused tugging on the cords, which were used to tie the cover down. Two weeks later the cords had already abraded the paint. It's ironic that the method used to protect the paint can cause damage instead.

Very inexpensive covers are likely to be quite thin. Some covers are so thin and have such a large weave that dirt and dust will filter right through them. Cheap covers probably won't fit snugly either; they usually come in only a few sizes. And in the case of plastic covers, they probably won't last very long in the sun. In fact, some plastic covers will become brittle and disintegrate after only a few months in the sun. They also tear easier.

However, inexpensive covers are sometimes the best choice, again, depending on the intended use. For example, if your car has to spend a few weeks in a body shop or garage, a cheap cover might provide the most economical protection for overspray, dirt, and grease.

Types of Fabrics

Cotton flannel fabrics breathe, allowing air to circulate through them. They are soft and easy on the car's paint and wax. They have no fluid resistance so they should only be used in the dry environment of a garage.

Cotton/polyester fabrics have poor fluid resistance and they trap heat and moisture. Their stiffness can harm your paint and remove wax, and they can also fade. When they are treated with a chemical repellent, they lose their ability to breathe. Nylon fabrics have the same deficiencies as cotton/polyester.

Plastic films should be avoided because they don't breathe, they trap heat and moisture, their stiffness can damage your paint, they shrink in the cold and stretch in the heat, and they provide only minimal hail and nick protection. Vinyl films should also be avoided when used outside for the same reasons.

Composite covers made from several layers of material combine the best qualities of each type. For example, covers made from Kimberly/Clark's Evolution 3 fabric is made in four layers which allow the cover to breathe, repel fluids, and provide protection against hail and nicks. Another benefit is that some covers will not rot or mildew if folded and stored while wet.

If you only plan to use a cover in the garage, then a cotton cover may be sufficient. If the car is kept outside or if it will be trailered, then a multi-layer fabric may provide the best means to keep the car's finish clean, dry, and scratch-free. For tips on how to correctly remove and install a car cover, turn the page.

1

2

CAR COVER PROCEDURE

Car covers should be removed and installed correctly. This not only makes putting it on easier, but it also helps prevent scratching the surface of the car. Begin by folding the front half over itself until you reach the middle of the roof (1). Repeat the procedure from the rear (2) and when the rear reaches the roof, fold the rear half over the front half. Finally, fold the passenger side up onto the roof, then fold the driver's side over it (3). The cover is now folded small enough to store easily, and by using the same system every time, you'll know which end is which when you place it back on the car and unfold it.

3

10

DETAILING AS A BUSINESS

Here's an example of a mobile rig that can be hitched to a small pickup or car. It belongs to Chad Heath, Technical Diirector for Eagle One. Chad estimates he has about $5000 invested in the rig.

The automotive detailing business has been around as long as there have been cars, and really began to grow after World War II. From that time through the 1980s, much of this business has been centered around an auto dealer having cars detailed for resale. It wasn't until the late 1980s that detailing began to grow as a consumer-oriented service. There are several reasons for this.

First, most people are keeping their cars much longer. Not only are today's cars engineered better, but they also cost a lot more. Second, average household incomes have risen at the expense of leisure time, and many people are willing to spend money to pay someone to detail their car rather than sacrifice what precious little free time they have.

As a result, detailing services are being offered in greater numbers at body shops, by dealerships, car washes, auto repair shops and even gas stations. Many of these businesses use independent contractors to offer these services. The detailing business today can be grouped into two broad categories: Maintenance and Restoration.

Maintenance services are done to relatively new vehicles or vehicles that have been well maintained. The services include washing, waxing and light interior shampooing. Restoration services involve maintenance services plus those services needed to restore an older vehicle to near showroom condition. This involves engine cleaning, hand cleaning of wheels, buffing, polishing and waxing of the paint and extensive cleaning and shampooing of the interior, top to bottom.

Many automatic car wash operations, for example, choose to offer the maintenance services because they require less equipment, less time and relatively unskilled personnel.

TYPE OF DETAILING BUSINESS

In addition to the type of service you want to offer, you have a choice in the type of detail business you want

This is a similar unit installed in the back of a truck. The equipment is the best quality but it's not as neatly organized as Chad's.

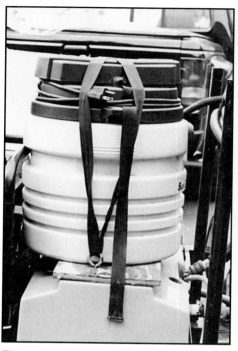

The wet-or-dry vacuum is attached to a platform mounted to the high-pressure washer. It's secured tightly with motorcycle tie-down straps.

The two storage boxes in the front of Chad's rig contain towels: one for cleaning and one for polishing. Each container has a separate pocket for soiled towels.

to operate—fixed location or mobile. Both have their advantages and disadvantages, and of course, vary widely in terms of initial investment.

Basic Equipment Needed

Whether operating a fixed or mobile detailing business, you will need the following list of equipment. Use this list and find the best prices in your area to determine the amount of money you'll need to get started. Home supply stores, such as Home Depot, carry some of these products, as do specialty automotive parts stores, especially big retail chains. Details on some of these products are covered in Chapter 1.

Pressure Washer—You should have one that can deliver no more than 1000 to 1500 psi of water.

Air Compressor—Don't skimp here. You'll be using it constantly if you have air-driven buffing tools, so get the best one you can afford. You'll need one from 3 hp to 15 hp.

Wet-Dry Vacuum—Get one with maximum suction, and a large capacity tank. Either a portable or central type will do.

Carpet/Upholstery Extractor—This may not be on your "must-have" list, but it is a tool that separates the amateurs from the pros. Get a heated one if possible.

High Speed Rotary Buffer—Either an electric or pneumatic will do. Remember, practice on something else rather than your first customer.

Orbital Polisher—An electric or pneumatic one will do.

Rotary Shampoo Machine—Optional, but great for deep carpet cleaning.

Chad uses a top-of-the-line Honda generator. Beside the obvious advantages of such a unit, it's very, very quiet. This is an important consideration, because he often works in residential neighborhoods.

Jason, who has a WashNet mobile detailing franchise, demonstrates the two-gallon wash job. Note the wand for reaching across the car. On careful inspection, you can see the fine mist of water flowing onto the car. This type of wash only works on lightly soiled, well-maintained cars that don't need a heavy washing. If you had to use a wash solution, then you'd need more water, but this system would still ration it out.

The big box on Chad's rig holds the chemicals, brushes and tools.

Buffing & Polishing Pads—Since most vehicles are clearcoated, get extra foam pads. Make sure you have pads with various cutting abilities, and that you have at least two of each.

Assorted Brushes—In this category, you'll need soft, medium and hard bristles, toothbrushes, cotton swabs, acid swabs.

Microfine Sandpapers—Assorted grits from 600 to 2000 grit for finessing defects.

Washing Tools—Again, several mitts (at least two), sponges, chamois and buckets.

Towels—Cotton terry cloth and nothing else. Get a bunch, you'll need them for buffing, polishing, windows, cleaning chemical residue in the engine compartment, etc. Some detailers color-code their towels, red for applying, blue for buffing, etc.

Chemicals—These are your lifeblood, and you should choose them with care. Although these products are covered in Chapter 1, I will present them here for review. Essentially, you need the following at minimum:

• Tires & Wheels: All purpose wheel cleaner, tire cleaner, tire protectant, wheel polish
• Car Wash Chemicals: Car wash shampoo, bug & tar remover, adhesive remover
• Trunk: Carpet shampoo, all purpose cleaner, tar & grease remover, spot remover, dressing, deodorizer
• Interior: Carpet & upholstery shampoo, extractor shampoo, spot remover, shampoo rinse, all purpose cleaner, window cleaner, leather cleaner and conditioner, vinyl cleaner and conditioner, deodorizer, and fabric protectant.
• Paint Finish: Heavy, medium and fine cleaners, fine polish and swirl remover, wax, wipe on/wipe off maintenance products (such as Meguiar's Quik Mist).
• Exterior: Chrome polish, glass cleaner, vinyl conditioner/cleaner, rubber restorer.

These are the basics. You'll be adding to this list as time and need warrant. Now, let's discuss the pros and cons of mobile and fixed location detailing.

Mobile Detailing

Probably the least expensive way to start in the business is to equip your own trailer or truck or van with the minimum amount of equipment and product necessary to offer

This very small fountain pump is all that's needed for the deionized water system WashNet uses. Compare this to Sid and Cathy's high-pressure washer on the big step-van.

If you aren't able to use the 2-gallon wash system, in many parts of the country you must put down a wash mat. This prevents any water run-off into the municipal sewer system or water ways. After the car is washed, the runoff is captured within the mat, collected and stored for proper disposal. Photo by Cathy White

maintenance detailing services. Mobile detailing is an especially viable alternative in sunbelt states, where the weather is favorable most of the time so you can work outside. As of this writing, it is possible to equip your own truck or van for about $2000 or so. Or, you could purchase a mobile detailing unit from someone who wants to get out of the business.

Disadvantages—There are, however, some disadvantages. First is the cost of maintenance on the rig, and the costs of traveling from location to location. Second, you need to have some method of waste containment and water reclamation; and third, you will experience difficulty in providing all the detailing services that someone may want because of space and equipment limitations.

Special Equipment Considerations—Aside from the list of basic equipment just described, mobile detailing does require first and foremost a reliable vehicle. A mobile rig should be truly mobile; you can't rely on a readily available water supply, so you'll have to bring it with

you. To get through several washes, you should have a tank with a 100 gallon capacity.

Mobile Franchises—Throughout the country, because of the great demand for detailing services, many entrepreneurs are developing franchised detailing services. For a lump sum you're fully equipped (on your truck or trailer) with all of the latest equipment, materials and supplies. Additionally, you're given full training not only in the use of the equipment, but in the techniques of detailing, and how to attract and keep customers.

Depending on how the franchiser works, you generally pay a small daily fee for materials and product. Sometimes this includes upkeep and maintenance of the equipment. Usually, if the equipment can't be repaired before you go out, the franchiser will loan you another piece of equipment so you won't have to cancel any customers. Some franchisers even bill and collect for you. If you're interested in buying a franchise, call WASHNET in Carlsbad, California, at (760) 929-2203 and ask for information.

Advanced Equipment—In some areas of Southern California, and I assume other parts of the country as well, run-off from mobile car washers is not allowed to flow into storm drains. To comply with these laws, new equipment has been developed and made available to the mobile detailer.

For the detailer using high pressure washers, a portable wash mat has been developed. This can be seen in the photo above. This device is made of reinforced, heavy duty plastic and can be folded into a convenient bundle and stored in your truck or trailer. When needed, it's unfolded and laid on the street or ground. The car is driven onto it and the 4 or 5-inch sides raised. Now, when the car is washed, all the dirty water is captured and held as a pool within the mat. This water is then sucked up with a vacuum and held in a disposal container. At the end of the day, the collected water is discharged into a collection station. Usually the collection station is at the local car wash. You pay a small fee for disposing of this wash water.

Another way of getting around the run-off problem is the newly

Cathy and Sid White are the owners and operators of this rig, which represents mobile detailing at its most professional. Notice that the bench in the right photo is actually a custom water tank. There is one on the other side as well. The Whites keep about one week to 10 days worth of supplies on board. Additionally, they have their own water deionizing system on board. Sid says that in the near future, everything you see here will be inside cabinets that are under construction.

developed two-gallon wash job. This requires two additional pieces of equipment. The first is a water deionizing system, which essentially removes all minerals from your water, the chief culprit of water spots. Eliminating these minerals means you'll be able to use less water.

Cathy White of Winners Circle Show Detail Specialists, explains that since there are no minerals in the deionized water, it wants to attract minerals to itself to bring it back into balance. Where are the minerals? In the dirt on the car. So, if there's no grease on the car, the deionized water will lift the dirt without a cleaning solution. Consequently, there's no rinsing to be done. Water on, wipe it off and you have a clean car using less than three gallons of water!

To use so little water requires a system different than that of the high pressure washer. Here, you buy a simple 110 volt water pump such as might be used in a garden fountain. This is attached to a much narrower hose than what we use in high

pressure work. For low pressure work an inside diameter of 3/8-inch is the standard. Of course, a smaller jet must be used at the end of the hose.

The well-equipped detailer will have a deionizing tank on board his rig, or one at home from which he can draw water. This will be coupled with a low pressure water system. However, it won't replace the high

pressure system which is a matter of necessity if you wish to do heavy-duty work such as detailing cars for the resale market.

The next piece of equipment to consider is a carpet cleaning machine.

This machine sprays a fine mist of cleaner over the carpet. You then scrub with a brush then go back and rinse and vacuum all with one tool

The Whites have this high pressure water system located on the other side of the truck.

The Whites have all of their heavy equipment, such as this 1.5 hp air compressor, mounted in lockers around the outside of the truck for easy access.

and at the same time. The result is a clean fabric surface that will dry in a couple of hours. On a full detail job, if you do the seats first, they'll be dry by the time the car is finished.

This is the perfect piece of equipment with which to shampoo carpets, cloth seats, convertible tops and all the fiber products within the vehicle. Again, this meets many of the Water Quality Resources Department's requirements of eliminating run-off into the storm drains. Although it's not as effective as flood-washing the carpet mats, it does a good job and saves hundreds, even thousands of gallons of water over a period of years. This is the piece of equipment you need if you plan to deliver a car with dry cloth seats the same day they were shampooed.

The Fixed Location

Many in the industry prefer not to be a mobile unit. They wish to establish a business location and stay there. In high traffic areas where many will see the operation, this can be very successful. This is usually where a detailer will wind up after

many years of being on the road. This is not necessarily a car wash, although it may be. What I'm talking about is a stationary detailing business where the customer comes to you. These are usually of two types: temporary and permanent.

Temporary Locations

Temporary locations are the small detail shops you find associated with a

gasoline filling station, parking garage, or under a large canvas awning in the parking lot of the local department store. Here, the detailer develops a business of drive-in customers. They see the business, and like any other retail outlet, drive in to have services performed.

The equipment in one of these locations is the same equipment you would have on your trailer or in your van. In fact, in Los Angeles, I know of three men who continue to work from their trailer but share space with other businesses. For you, it's far more convenient than running from one customer to the next. For the customer, however, it's a little less convenient, and they expect to pay less. The fact that they may have to leave their car for several hours is also not practical.

One suggestion is to offer a pick-up and delivery service. Many customers are willing to pay a bit more for this added convenience.

With a stationary business in either a temporary or permanent location,

Don and George Kordyak converted a junkyard in San Bernardino into one of the best detailing shops in Southern California. The fact this was once a junkyard meant that the area had drawn automotive clientele for years. They have over 8 bays.

The waste water from the Kordyak's shop runs off the car and into this filtration system below. Here, sand filters out the harmful products and clean waste water runs to the sewer system. This is one of the advantages of a permanent installation. Twice a year the water resources department comes around to check the filter and make sure it's working properly. The rest of the time there's no hassle.

however, you give a greater impression of stability.

Permanent Locations

This is like any other traditional business, where you go and find a suitable location with good traffic and in the right market, then renovate it to suit your detailing business. In such a building, the detailer has everything confined within a lot and building. Equipment is protected. Work can be performed even in bad weather. There is a waiting room for customers and an office to deal with trades people. The suppliers come to you. Telephones are at your elbow to stay in touch with customers and suppliers. Any waste water or hazardous waste problems were solved in the early stages of setting up the business and no longer present a worry or a problem. Insurance costs are less because everything can be locked up. Workman's compensation is less expensive because working conditions are safer. The benefits are endless—as are the responsibilities.

With a large stationary detailing

business, it is possible to expand as your business grows. You have the option of adding services such as paintless dent repairs, minor paint and body work, engine tune-ups, oil changes and lube, and so on.

BUSINESS DETAILS

One chapter of one book is insufficient to turn you into a fully competent business person. I can show you the steps, point you in the right direction, and make the start-up process easy for you. You must, however, educate yourself further. You bought this book to polish your skills in the ways to detail a car. Now you must acquire other books that will hone your business skills. Keeping a customer's car the cleanest it has ever been is only one part of being in business. What I can do is give you some general pointers on some of the "details" you'll have to consider to establish a business.

Licenses & Permits

The city, county, state, and federal

governments all want to know what you're doing, why you're doing it, and where it's being done. Therefore, each requires a license. The requirements for obtaining a license vary from region to region. Some require that you demonstrate your knowledge with a certificate or some other form of proof, while others require that you simply fill out an application and pay a fee. The latter is much more the case for detailing.

Begin your licensing quest at your local city administration building or offices. Every city or town in the United States has these offices and the address and phone number can be found in the phone book. If you live in an unincorporated area (not a city or town) begin your application at the county administration. They'll check for you to see with whom you must apply and direct you to those offices.

Getting a business license, sometimes called a business permit, is really very easy. Usually you fill out a form, pay a small fee, and are issued a temporary license while waiting for the new one. Usually you must display your license or permit where it can be seen by the general public.

As a mobile detailer this is a bit hard to do. I suggest you take the permit to a good stationers or trophy shop and have it laminated between two sheets of plastic. Keep it in your glove compartment for presentation should anyone ask to see it.

Water Resources Department

Every community, large or small, has a different set of rules and regulations when it comes to water, especially waste water.

When you apply for your city license, the department clerk should

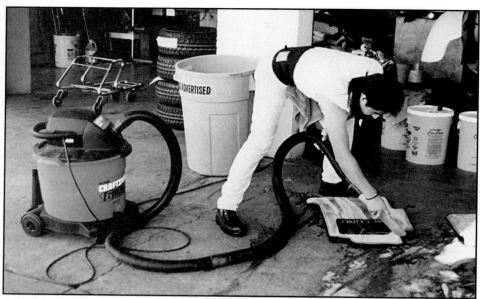

If you're going to have employees, be prepared for a mountain of paperwork, most of it concerning taxes. The best advice is to hire a professional, like an accountant, to take care of these details.

direct you to the water department. If he or she doesn't, ask to be directed. Don't think because he didn't say anything, there are no requirements. It's your responsibility, and, if you break any laws, you won't be let off the hook with the excuse that you didn't know you were doing something wrong. So be sure you're in complete compliance with all your community's waste water discharge regulations.

State Tax Boards

In California the department charged with collecting state sales tax is the State Board of Equalization. In California, we do not tax services and so, as a service provider, you're not responsible to collect sales tax on your service. Now, if you add a product line to your business, those products are subject to taxation. Such products could be those little air fresheners that hang from the rear view mirror. Perhaps your customer wants a few gallons of chemical to send to his sister in another state.

Sales taxes would be due.

These are the rules in California. Your state may have different ones. Again, while you're applying for your license or permit, ask the clerk where your local state taxing authority offices are and give them a call. You don't even have to go in, everything can be done over the phone. It is my understanding that few states tax services, but find out if this is so in your state.

Internal Revenue Services

The IRS has no licensing or permits, but nonetheless you must be prepared to deal with them. If you become an employer, you must have an employee identification number and withhold federal taxes from your employees' wages. This is a long and complex application and should be followed through with your local agent.

Your individual relationship to the IRS is to let them know you've started a business. In turn, they'll send you tax forms that "allow" you to pay

taxes on your income (from your business) each quarter rather than all at once at the end of the year.

Your relationship to the IRS is one of those areas which require further reading and studying as I mentioned above, and I strongly recommend that you hire a professional.

Insurance

You must insure yourself and your business. This is going to be one of your largest expenses but one which, should you avoid, could cost you everything for the rest of your life.

Liability Insurance—Of the insurance you must have, liability insurance gives you the most protection. Business liability insurance protects you in case you injure someone or someone's property. The first and easiest example is burning through a customer's paint (it's always on a new Mercedes—never an old Ford) with a buffer and being responsible for several thousand dollars in repairs. A good attorney can get his client a complete new paint job for your 1-inch burn. Let the insurance company worry about it.

What if your customer gets her hair caught in your compressor? This has happened. You're driving your customer's car and you hit a pedestrian. Your generator goes bad, leaks gas and burns up all your equipment and your truck, too. The fire spreads to the business next to where you parked your rig. The business goes up in flames.

Yes, some of this is far fetched, but it happens, so don't play the odds—get adequate liability insurance.

My suggestion for insurance is this: Buy two policies—one to insure your business and one to insure your

As a business, you'll need to establish a relationship with a good supplier so you can purchase in bulk, on credit. Auto Magic and Meguiar's both cater to the professional detailer.

personal vehicle. These will be in addition to such policies as homeowners or renters insurance, life insurance, workman's comp you may buy when you have employees, or any health plans. Liability insurance should have a minimum of $300,000. The deductibles (the part of the claim you must pay out of your pocket) should be no more than $1000–$5000. Then, buy a million dollar umbrella policy. Umbrella policies protect you beyond the limits of your liability insurance.

Comprehensive Insurance—If you buy liability insurance you automatically get comprehensive (although you pay extra). Comprehensive insurance covers everything that liability does not. If in the rig fire, all that was lost was your rig and no other property was damaged or people injured, your comprehensive insurance would pay you for the rig— less whatever deductible you elected.

Record Keeping

Being in business requires extensive record keeping. At the very minimum for a mobile detailing operation, you must answer to the tax collector and keep track of all income and expenses, like product purchases, vehicle mileage and maintenance, fuel, and even labor, even if it is part-time. If your supplier says you failed to pay your June invoice, you should have a copy of the canceled check to prove otherwise. You may be wise to include a computer system with a simple money management system like Quicken for a small, one man mobile detailing operation. For fixed location with employees and overhead, the record-keeping is much more extensive, and having an automated computer system is almost a necessity.

Expense Receipts—Every cent you spend for your business may be deducted from what the business earns and is consequently not taxed. This includes all your chemicals, the cost of buying water (whether or not it's deionized), your business cards, stationery, fliers, advertisements, and anything you do to attract customers (this falls under advertising). If you must take a potential client to lunch, part of the lunch is tax deductible. All

of the expenses associated with driving are deductible. This can be figured on a "per mile" basis or you can save all your receipts from gas, oil, tires, repairs, and anything else spent for your vehicle as it relates to your business. You can't, however, claim pleasure driving as a business expense.

Every single item you purchase for your business should come with a receipt. If the clerk fails to give you one, ask for it. These receipts must be saved. Then, once a month, you or your accountant must log them into a book under a column titled "expenses."

Income Receipts—Every time you sell a service or product to a customer, you must give them a receipt—just as you received a receipt for the money you spent. Each receipt you make will have at least two copies: one for your customer (who may be able to deduct it as a business expense) and one copy you keep.

After the last day of the month, or when all records are in for that month, subtract the total "expenses" from total "income."

By keeping these excellent records you always know where you are. You know if you're earning money or losing money. If every day you throw away your receipts and spend whatever money you have, you don't really know where you are. And, as we all know, if you spend money that should be going to pay bills, you wind up in big, big trouble.

What has just been described here in its most basic form is the practice of bookkeeping. It's something you can easily do yourself if you take the time to learn. As I said, there are several wonderful, easy to use computer programs that automate all of this after some simple setup.

Taxes—Yet another part of good record keeping is to be able to know how much tax you owe on your quarterly tax payments. In a similar manner you'll compute your state taxes and social security tax. If any of them are late, you'll be fined (quite heavily) and charged interest for the period they remain unpaid. It's in your own best interest then to keep accurate records, set aside money for taxes in a separate bank account, and run your business in the most professional way possible. Again, seek the advice of a professional unless you really know what you are doing.

Customer Record Keeping—As important as it is to keep good records of your income and expenses, it's equally important to keep good records about your customers, their preferences and payment history. For each customer you serve, you should have a book wherein you keep their name, address, phone number and the service you perform for them. Additionally, there should be a place for entering what you charge them on a daily, weekly or monthly basis. Another column should be devoted to when they paid and how much.

Marketing

Today, as in the past, dealer business is probably the easiest to find. All you need to do is contact the used car lots or the used car manager of the dealership to solicit business. Bear in mind, however, there are a lot of detailers out there competing for this work, all ready to cut prices to get the business. That is why dealer prices remain so low.

The retail business, while much more lucrative, is more difficult to find. Some key factors to remember when marketing your detail services to a consumer are:

• The type of car they drive
• Their profession
• The neighborhood in which they live

Direct Mail & Flyers—The best forms of advertising you can use to reach these types of customers have proven to be direct mail or flyer distribution in the neighborhood. You may be able to purchase mailing lists by vehicle make and zip code from your local Department of Motor Vehicles. A mailing service can supply you mailing lists by profession and by neighborhood.

Flyers distributed on vehicles in neighborhoods or shopping center parking lots usually land some customers. Remember, with these customers, quality and service is more important than price. They will be less motivated by coupons or discount than by an educational advertising message. Tell them you shampoo and clean interiors and polish and wax paint.

Prices should be quoted only after seeing the vehicles and determining the needs. However, before advertising to the general public, let your current customer base know that you now offer detailing services and what they are. You will be amazed at how much business this will generate from existing customers, friends and relatives.

I would like to suggest two very excellent books on the subject that you should add to your business library and read at least once a year. They are: *Guerrilla Marketing* (Secrets for Making Big Profits from your Small Business), and *Guerrilla Marketing for the Home-Based Business.*

Both are by Jay Levinson and are available at any of the large, chain bookstores. If you must order them through a store where they're not carried on the shelf, order *Guerrilla Marketing* using the ISBN number 0-395-64496-8. *Guerrilla Marketing for the Home-Based Business* is ISBN 0-395-74283-8. Both books are published by Houghton/Mifflin.

The thing that makes these two books stand out from the rest is that they are directed to the individual with very little capital resources (money). They give the reader hundreds of ideas about finding customers that cost little or no money.

WHERE TO GET ADVICE

If you are serious about setting up a detail business, you should get the advice of a professional consultant. R.L. "Bud" Abraham, who contributed some of the information that appears in this chapter, owns Detail Plus Car Appearance Systems in Portland, Oregon. Detail Plus is a manufacturer of detailing equipment, supplies and chemicals. The company also conducts training seminars and provides detailing business consulting. For more information, contact Detail Plus, 12849 NE Airport Way, Portland, OR 97230. Tel: 503/251-2955.

PAINT

1. What is gloss?

A: Gloss is an optical characteristic that describes the capacity of a surface to reflect directed light. A high gloss paint surface is one that directly reflects light with minimum hazing or diffusion. Dirt and grime on the surface of a car's paint absorb and diffuse light making it look dull and lifeless. No paint will remain glossy if it is neglected—even the new so-called "no-wax" paints that still are exposed to the same environmental contamination as all other paint.

Proper paint care is one of the most rewarding activities you can do. Not only do you instantly see a difference, but when it comes time to sell or trade in your car, it will be worth far more than a similar model that has been neglected.

2. Why do car finishes fade? What is oxidation? How can I prevent it from happening?

A: Automotive paint is designed to reflect light which creates those dazzling shines seen in most new car showrooms. If your car was washed daily and kept indoors most of the day, the shine would last for years because there would be no surface contamination to dull, stain or oxidize the finish.

Most modern car finishes consist of a base coating that contains the color and 2 protective coats. Clearcoating on top is designed to protect the color paint from oxidizing. This outer clearcoat adds UV protection that helps prevent the sun's rays from drying out the base paint. Oxidation was an obvious problem ten years ago because you quickly saw the color fade. Now that the outer paint layer is usually clear, oxidation is less obvious...yet it still occurs. The sun

dries out the top paint layers and natural oils are lost. If these oils aren't replaced, the paint oxidizes and the surface gradually becomes duller and duller.

Today's clearcoat finishes especially look faded whenever the surface becomes contaminated by airborne pollution, acid rain, industrial fallout and countless other factors. If the contamination isn't removed frequently, it reduces the reflective quality of the finish and it can look dull and lifeless. If the contamination is left on the car for some time, it can begin to etch into the thin color coat paint layer and expose the base coat to direct UV rays and even greater damage. Once the clearcoat protection is gone, the car usually requires costly repainting.

3. What is clearcoat? How can I tell if I have it?

A: Today, most modem car finishes consist of a base coating of paint that contains the color pigments and a protective clearcoating on top that is designed to protect the color from oxidizing. This outer clearcoat paint will protect the color as long as it is maintained properly and isn't damaged. An easy way to tell if you have a clearcoat is by looking at your applicator when polishing or waxing. If you see color on the applicator of buffing material, you do not have a clearcoat. Clearcoat paints require special care and you should never use harsh abrasive waxes or rubbing compounds on them.

4. What is the difference between a polish and a wax?

A: Today there is a lot of confusion about the difference between a polish and wax. Many manufacturers are marketing waxes as "polishes" and the terms have become almost inter-changeable.

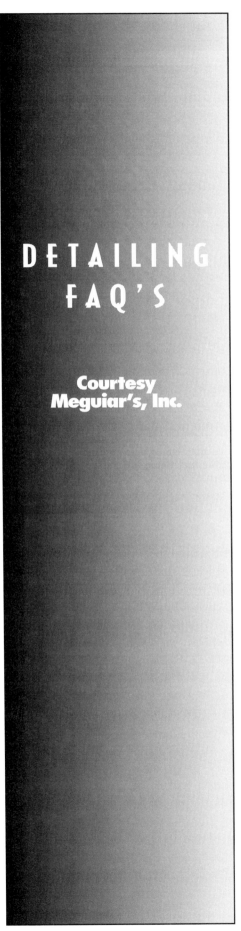

DETAILING
FAQ'S

Courtesy
Meguiar's, Inc.

Professionals know there is a big difference. A pure polish is more like a paint conditioner that restores valuable oils to the paint and eliminates fine scratches and creates incredible high gloss that would not be possible with a wax. An application of a pure polish should be followed by waxing to protect the shine and extend it. If you own a dark color car, you'll see a dramatic difference if you use a polish.

5. Are polymer sealants good for my car?

A: Quality polymer sealants are noted for their long lasting abilities, but in recent years there have been many inferior formulations marketed at extremely high prices. These products are mostly hype and lull a car owner into thinking one application will last for years—only to discover later that their finish has been damaged by a lack of care.

6. What is carnauba wax?

A: Carnauba wax comes from a species of palm trees in South America and is one of the hardest types of wax available. It works best when it is properly blended with other waxes so it becomes easier to apply and buff off. It is also best applied after an application of a pure polish.

7. Are waxes with Teflon any good?

A: Some professionals consider "Teflon" formulas as empty hype. Even the maker of Teflon (DuPont) issued the following statement:

"The addition of a Teflon flouro-polymer resin does nothing to enhance the properties of a car wax. We have no data that indicates the use of Teflon is beneficial in car waxes."

8. What about colored waxes that match my car's paint?

A: First, there are thousands of car colors used every year. Some paint companies offer over one hundred different reds. There is no way that a limited selection of 12 different color waxes can match your color exactly.

Second, most paints today have a top layer of paint that is clear—it does not contain the color pigments. If you add a pigmented wax on top of the clear surface, you are creating an unnatural effect that will look even stranger as the pigments in the paint fade. Picture applying shoe polish to your windshield and you can picture what is happening when you apply color waxes to clearcoat paint.

If you want a great finish and to hide scratches, it is best to use quality cleaners, pure polishes, and waxes that restore the surface properly.

9. What is the difference between washing and cleaning?

A: Washing is the process of loosening surface dirt and grime on a car's paint. Cleaning is a separate process that we like to call "deep cleaning" because it is designed to safely remove dead, oxidized paint as well as stubborn surface contamination that does not come off easily during washing (i.e. acid rain stains).

Paint that has been neglected or that has undergone severe environmental contamination should be first washed then deep cleaned with a mild abrasive product that is safe on all paints. Once the surface has been cleaned, it should then be nourished with an application of a pure polish, then protected with an application of a quality wax. Those with dark colors will only achieve incredible results if applying the pure polish before waxing.

A good key point to remember when cleaning is that you always want to start with the least abrasive method possible. It would be foolish to go straight to a compound to take out a problem. First, try a fine abrasive cleaner, then work your way to more abrasive products. If you have serious surface problems, it is usually best to have a professional detailer do the job.

10. What causes swirl marks? How do I remove them—especially on dark cars?

A: Swirl marks are caused by micro scratches on the finish often caused by the use of a buffer with the wrong type of polishing pad and/or wax/polish. Hand applications that appear to leave swirl marks (especially on dark colors) are often just smudges or streaks from faulty application techniques or an inferior wax/polish.

If you use a buffer for personal use of application of waxes, it is recommended that you only use an orbital buffer since an orbital buffer runs in an eccentric motion that greatly reduces swirling. There is less danger of the buffer scratching the paint than with rotary buffers.

If you have light swirls, you can use a cleaner/wax from a quality company, or a swirl remover to safely restore the finish. If you have deep swirls, you will probably have to first use a safe paint cleaner, followed by a pure polish, then a protective wax. If this process won't remove the swirl marks, you will need to take your car to a local professional to see if the scratches are so deep that high speed buffing or possibly painting is needed.

11. How do I get rid of stains, spots, and smears on my car?

A: If at all possible, it is best to get

any contamination off of the car, before it becomes a problem. You can do this with a mist-n-wipe product made specifically for this purpose. If the stain or spot becomes imbedded in the paint, you will need to clean the surface and remove the contamination, using the methods in Chapter 4.

12. What can I do to hide small scratches in my car's paint?

A: If you are like most car owners, you have a clearcoat paint on your car and small scratches are magnified. This paint layer is clear and scratches refract the color base coat layer below. Don't be fooled by claims that color matched waxes can hide these scratches. Since your surface paint is clear, pigmented wax will look strange and won't do the job.

If your scratches are small, the use of a pure polish prior to frequent waxing is the best way to hide the scratches. The polish will restore valuable oils to the damaged paint and will reduce the optical refraction that makes those scratches noticeable.

13. How long does a car wax last? Would it last longer if I applied two or three coats?

A: There is no standard answer to how long a car wax will last. There are many variables that influence the life of the wax:

• Type and color of paint
• Condition of the paint
• Local environment (normal and extraordinary)
• Number of hours kept outdoors
• Quality of the wax used and method of application
• How often the car is washed, hand/car wash

Applying two or three coats of wax at one time can give some extra protection on the most critical areas (hood, front areas). Generally, the coat should be sufficient for the entirety of the vehicle. It would be in your best interest to do it more frequently.

Environmental conditions today demand more frequent waxing to prevent costly damage to the outer layers of paint.

14. How often should I wax my car?

A: There is no standard answer to how often you should wax. The answer to this question would be similar to the answer of the last question. The different factors determine how frequently you would need to wax.

Beading of water is not always necessarily an indication of the wax protection. Some of the newer car washes are designed not to bead on the paint, but rather to sheet off the surface making it easier to dry. In that case, running your clean hand along the surface of your car, you should be able to tell if the surface is slick or rough. A rough surface usually means it needs cleaning, but most definitely means it needs more wax protection.

15. Why do I have to wax so often? With today's paint technology, I thought waxing was no longer necessary?

A: In addition to countless environmental factors, catalytic emissions out of the cars in front of you are sending out hydrochloric and/or sulfuric acid particles that land on your car's upper surfaces. All of these contaminants take a toll on your car's paint if not properly maintained.

Can you imagine what would happen if you only brushed your teeth once a year? The build up could lead to costly repairs and you might never get your teeth looking as good as they did before.

Your car's paint is constantly exposed to the elements and needs regular care to keep it looking its best.

If you neglect your car, a good paint job could cost $4,000. If you decide to sell your car without a new paint job, it could cost you anywhere between $500 and $5,000 in lost trade-in value depending upon the age and type of your car. "You can expect from $500 to $5,000 more at resale time from a well detailed, sharp-looking vehicle instead of one that's "showing its age."

16. How can I tell if my car needs waxing or polishing?

A: Clearcoat paints make it more difficult to determine when your car needs waxing or polishing. It may need it far sooner than it looks like it needs it. Here are two tests to tell if your car needs attention:

Wad a clean, dry terry cloth towel and rub it along a clean upper surface of your car. If you hear squeaking, that's a sure sign you need a wax.

After washing and drying your car, take your hand and run your palm along the upper surfaces of your car's hood and trunk. If you detect rough spots or feel drag, you also know you need a wax—and probably a cleaner if the problem is more severe.

17. Do waxes have Ultraviolet (UV) protection?

A: Some waxes do contain UVprotection agents, but the amount of protection is limited. The main goal of a wax is to protect the upper layers of paint that do contain UV protection agents. If your car is waxed regularly, your paint will be protected and you should suffer no major UV damage.

18. Will I get better results by hand or with a buffer?

A: Professionals prefer using an orbital buffer because it makes it faster and easier to apply the right amount of even pressure during the application and buffing process. Often hand application or buffing creates uneven pressure—especially if the wrong applicator or buffing material is used.

Anyone waxing by hand should always use thick deep-pile terry cloth toweling for buffing. This protects the paint and helps prevent uneven buffing. Avoid putting pressure on tops of ridges where your paint is the thinnest.

19. What is the difference between an orbital polisher and a rotary buffer?

A: An orbital buffer runs in an eccentric circular motion. It is never in the same place at the same time like your hand or a regular rotary buffer. An orbital buffer doesn't apply torque to the surface and uses a random pattern to safely do its job.

If you use a rotary buffer and are not skilled in its use, you could easily apply too much pressure to the paint and burn right through it creating a need for a new paint job. Unless you are using the new technology with the foam buffing pads, and are trained for the use, it is best to avoid them. Buffers attached to power drills are unsafe for the same reasons.

A good orbital buffer will cost $120- $180 and should last for many years. Look for a model that runs at a minimum of 2200 rpm and has a 10-11" face pad. Black and Decker produces some high quality buffers.

20. What's the best wax to use on a brand new car? How soon can I begin waxing?

A: The best wax to use on a new car varies by the type of car you are buying, the environmental conditions in your area, and the amount of time you are willing to invest in waxing each year. A new car will require a non-abrasive wax that is safe for newer paints.

21. Should I use a non-silicone wax?

A: If your car needs repainting, silicone-based waxes create extra work for the painter. The wax will have to be stripped to avoid "fish-eye" problems in the painting process. The silicone embeds itself into the paint and new paint won't adhere properly.

The use of some silicone does make certain wax formulas easier to spread. There are good silicones and bad silicones. Some are good and necessary to achieve the best finish on a paint surface.

22. What's the best way to apply wax?

A: First, start with a quality wax. Your finish is valuable and it doesn't pay to use cheap inferior waxes... especially with the need for protection from environmental contamination. Apply the wax with a foam applicator and try to spread it evenly using gentle circular motions. If you prefer to apply by machine, only use an orbital buffer and be sure the wax was designed to work with a power buffer.

For buffing, only use a thick, high quality, cotton terry cloth toweling. Diapers, T shirts, thin toweling and other materials should not be used since they can harm the finish by dragging microscopic dirt particles across the paint. Thick, terry cloth toweling lifts the dirt particles off the surface and traps them in the toweling thereby leaving the finish smoother and richer.

Use only minimal amounts of fabric softener when cleaning terry cloth because it adds chemicals to the toweling and changes the performance. Sometimes it helps to throw a pre-used Bounce into the dryer. When applying wax, most quality formulas allow you to apply the wax to the entire car before buffing. This ensures that the wax has time to properly dry. CAUTION: Never apply wax to a hot surface. Work in a cool, shady area

23. Which is better—liquid or paste wax?

A: Thanks to recent technology advances, many liquid formulations will last as long as paste waxes. The real key is selecting the right quality formulations for your car.

24. What's the best way to wash a car?

A: First, do not use household detergents. These detergents were designed to strip off grease and grime and can actually strip off some of your wax protection and accelerate oxidation. Use quality car wash products that are pH balanced to gently clean your car.

Second, use a large bucket (at least 5 gallons) so that dirt particles sink to the bottom and the fresh suds you apply are free of major contamination. Some people may want to use two buckets—one for rinsing and one for the suds.

Third, make sure your car is in the shade, and hose the entire car down starting at the top. Apply suds to the upper areas first using thick terry toweling (it is better than a sponge because it safely lifts off dirt particles that can cause scratches). You might find that you have less water to dry off your car if you stream the water from the hose rather than use a sprayer.

Fourth, once your entire car is washed and rinsed, take a clean, dry terry cloth towel and wipe the car down starting at the top. Terry toweling is recommended over a chamois because of the tiny dirt particles still on the surface. The improper use of a chamois could result in scratching. The deep fingers in terry towels trap these particles and minimize the chance of scratching.

When drying, remember to keep your towel "flat" to the surface. Folding it into quarters gives you eight clean working surfaces.

25. Should I go to automatic car washes?

A: Automatic car washes vary greatly. Some are better than others. Avoid any automatic car washes that use brushes and drying materials which can scratch the paint finish. Also, be careful about car washes with poor water recycling systems and harsh soaps.

If you have a dark color car, it usually is best to have your car washed by hand. Dark colors quickly show small scratches.

26. How good are waxes sprayed on car washes?

A: Because these waxes have to be diluted with water to be sprayed on your car, you are getting minimal protection. Not to mention, if it was durable, the wax would be visible on your windows. It is far better to apply your wax by hand to insure maximum protection. Plus if you use a one-step cleaner/wax, it will also deep clean the paint and remove contamination and oxidation. These things cannot be removed by an automatic car wash.

27. What is acid rain?

A: Emissions from chemical plants, fossil fuel burning power plants, and the internal combustion engine are transported and altered in our atmosphere.

When deposited onto your car's surface in a dry state it may seem like simple dust but mix it with a little bit of dew, sprinklers, or rainfall, and you now have a mixture of sulfuric acid on your paint finish. Left on the surface for any period of time, and especially if placed in the direct sunlight, you now have etching on your paint finish. Typical acid rain damage may first look like water droplets which have dried on the paint and caused discoloration. In some cases, damage appears as a white ring with a dull center. Severe cases show pitting.

Depending on the level of defect, you will need to use a cleaner to restore the finish accordingly. In many cases, a professional high speed buffing job is the only way to remove the problem.

28. How can I keep acid rain, diesel exhaust and hard water from attaching to my car's paint?

A: This is a daily battle and the question cannot be answered without asking how often you are willing to spend taking care of your car. A simple mist-n-wipe product can save a lot of time and leave your finish in a beautiful state. The faster you can remove the contamination, the better.

LEATHER, RUBBER, VINYL, CANVAS

29. How do I remove wax on my rubber trim and bumpers?

A: First, try a simple mist-n-wipe product and wipe the surface down with a terry cloth towel. If the wax stain remains: "Microwave peanut butter, agitate with soft toothbrush—peanut butter dissolves the wax and the abrasiveness of peanut butter lifts stains off."

30. What should I use on my tires?

A: The secret to good looking tires is to clean the tire—not just shine the tire. Most silicone emulsion protectants cover over the surface contamination with a shiny coating that can cause discoloration and decay in the long run.

Professionals use a product that cleans, conditions and protects the vinyl or rubber. This leaves the surface looking like new, not like it's been coated in shiny plastic.

31. How should I care for my car's interior?

A: Interiors take a beating. Ultraviolet rays, heat build up, sliding in and out of seats, spilling of sodas, hauling objects, temperature extremes—all interior care is important. You should clean and protect your interior as often as you wash.

For dashboards and vinyl seating, use a quality protectant that cleans and protects. Most popular protectants do not clean the surface and end up covering over dirt. Some leave your surfaces greasy and slippery. Take care when choosing an interior product to avoid the ones that leave this type of finish.

For leather seats, only use special products designed for automotive seats. You especially want to find one with a nice leather aroma that restores the surface without changing its color.

For carpets and fabric seating, use only quality cleaners and repellents. To remove lint from fabric upholstery, wrap some duct tape around your hand (sticky side out) and gently tap against the upholstery.

32. How do you clean a car cover?

A: Covers vary and you should first consult the manufacturer for directions for the cover you have. You do not want to lose any of the water repellent qualities of the cover. Many covers can be washed in a laundromat using Ivory dish soap.

WINDOWS

33. How do I clean my tinted windows without damaging them?

A: Tinted windows require special care. They need to be treated as a clear plastic surface. We recommend a product specifically made for this application such as Mirror Glaze No. 18, Clear Plastic Cleaner/Polish because it is safe, restores optical clarity, and its anti-static formula repels dust that can be attracted to the tinting.

METAL

34. What is the best way to remove brake dust from my wheels?

A: Most newer aluminum wheels are clearcoated to stay bright and shiny. Brake dust will build up on top of the clearcoat so the challenge is to remove the brake dust without removing the clearcoat. To do this we recommend only using a spray-on wheel product that is designed for clearcoat wheels. It will loosen and suspend the brake dust particles and safely remove them without damaging the wheel's coating. Never use abrasive cleaners or brushes that could cut through the clearcoat protection.

Do not let brake dust build-up last more than two or three weeks to prevent etching into the surface.

35. Is there a safe polish that will not harm the metal, but will clean and polish safely?

A: There are several metal polishes on the market. Beware of those that contain abrasives.

Don Taylor has been restoring and writing about cars for several decades. An avid enthusiast and highly respected paint and body expert, he is one of HPBooks most prolific authors, having written or co-written HP's: Paint & Body Handbook; Mustang Restoration Handbook; Rebuild Big-Block Mopar Engines; and Rebuild Small-Block Mopar Engines. He lives in Fallbrook, California.

OTHER BOOKS FROM HPBOOKS AUTOMOTIVE

HANDBOOKS
Auto Electrical Handbook: 0-89586-238-7
Auto Upholstery & Interiors: 1-55788-265-7
Brake Handbook: 0-89586-232-8
Car Builder's Handbook: 1-55788-278-9
Street Rodder's Handbook: 0-89586-369-3
Turbo Hydra-matic 350 Handbook: 0-89586-051-1
Welder's Handbook: 1-55788-264-9

BODYWORK & PAINTING
Automotive Detailing: 1-55788-288-6
Automotive Paint Handbook: 1-55788-291-6
Fiberglass & Composite Materials: 1-55788-239-8
Metal Fabricator's Handbook: 0-89586-870-9
Paint & Body Handbook: 1-55788-082-4
Sheet Metal Handbook: 0-89586-757-5

INDUCTION
Holley 4150: 0-89586-047-3
Holley Carburetors, Manifolds & Fuel Injection: 1-55788-052-2
Rochester Carburetors: 0-89586-301-4
Turbochargers: 0-89586-135-6
Weber Carburetors: 0-89586-377-4

PERFORMANCE
Aerodynamics For Racing & Performance Cars: 1-55788-267-3
Baja Bugs & Buggies: 0-89586-186-0
Big-Block Chevy Performance: 1-55788-216-9
Big Block Mopar Performance: 1-55788-302-5
Bracket Racing: 1-55788-266-5
Brake Systems: 1-55788-281-9
Camaro Performance: 1-55788-057-3
Chassis Engineering: 1-55788-055-7
Chevrolet Power: 1-55788-087-5
Ford Windsor Small-Block Performance: 1-55788-323-8
Honda/Acura Performance: 1-55788-324-6
High Performance Hardware: 1-55788-304-1
How to Build Tri-Five Chevy Trucks ('55-'57): 1-55788-285-1
How to Hot Rod Big-Block Chevys:0-912656-04-2
How to Hot Rod Small-Block Chevys:0-912656-06-9
How to Hot Rod Small-Block Mopar Engines: 0-89586-479-7
How to Hot Rod VW Engines:0-912656-03-4
How to Make Your Car Handle:0-912656-46-8
John Lingenfelter: Modifying Small-Block Chevy: 1-55788-238-X
Mustang 5.0 Projects: 1-55788-275-4

Mustang Performance ('79–'93): 1-55788-193-6
Mustang Performance 2 ('79–'93): 1-55788-202-9
1001 High Performance Tech Tips: 1-55788-199-5
Performance Ignition Systems: 1-55788-306-8
Performance Wheels & Tires: 1-55788-286-X
Race Car Engineering & Mechanics: 1-55788-064-6
Small-Block Chevy Performance: 1-55788-253-3

ENGINE REBUILDING
Engine Builder's Handbook: 1-55788-245-2
Rebuild Air-Cooled VW Engines: 0-89586-225-5
Rebuild Big-Block Chevy Engines: 0-89586-175-5
Rebuild Big-Block Ford Engines: 0-89586-070-8
Rebuild Big-Block Mopar Engines: 1-55788-190-1
Rebuild Ford V-8 Engines: 0-89586-036-8
Rebuild Small-Block Chevy Engines: 1-55788-029-8
Rebuild Small-Block Ford Engines:0-912656-89-1
Rebuild Small-Block Mopar Engines: 0-89586-128-3

RESTORATION, MAINTENANCE, REPAIR
Camaro Owner's Handbook ('67–'81): 1-55788-301-7
Camaro Restoration Handbook ('67–'81): 0-89586-375-8
Classic Car Restorer's Handbook: 1-55788-194-4
Corvette Weekend Projects ('68-'82): 1-55788-218-5
Mustang Restoration Handbook('64 1/2–'70): 0-89586-402-9
Mustang Weekend Projects ('64-'67): 1-55788-230-4
Mustang Weekend Projects 2 ('68-'70): 1-55788-256-8
Tri-Five Chevy Owner's ('55-'57): 1-55788-285-1

GENERAL REFERENCE
Auto Math:1-55788-020-4
Fabulous Funny Cars: 1-55788-069-7
Guide to GM Muscle Cars: 1-55788-003-4
Stock Cars!: 1-55788-308-4

MARINE
Big-Block Chevy Marine Performance: 1-55788-297-5

HPBOOKS ARE AVAILABLE AT BOOK AND SPECIALTY RETAILERS OR TO
ORDER CALL: 1-800-788-6262, ext. 1

HPBooks
A division of Penguin Putnam Inc.
375 Hudson Street
New York, NY 10014